UNSUNG HEROES
OF THE MAJOR LEAGUES

Action-packed profiles of ten baseball stars whose unique contributions to their teams often went unnoticed. Included are Joe Rudi, Doug Rader, Phil Niekro, Thurman Munson, Cookie Rojas, Billy Williams, Mike Cuellar, Bill Melton, Ron Fairly, and Tony Perez.

illustrated with photographs

UNSUNG HEROES
OF THE MAJOR LEAGUES

BY ART BERKE

RANDOM HOUSE   NEW YORK

MAJOR LEAGUE
LIBRARY

Library of Congress Cataloging in Publication Data
Berke, Art.   Unsung heroes of the major leagues.   (Major league library)
CONTENTS: Joe Rudi.—Tony Perez.—Thurman Munson. [etc.]   Includes index.
1. Baseball—Biography—Juvenile literature. [1. Baseball—Biography] I. Title.
GV865.A1B47   796.357′092′2 [B] [920]   75-34909
ISBN 0-394-83096-2   ISBN 0-394-93096-7 lib. bdg.

Manufactured in the United States of America   1 2 3 4 5 6 7 8 9 0

PHOTOGRAPH CREDITS: John E. Biever, 16, 93, 118–119; Clifton Boutelle, 2, 7, 13,
39, 65, 79, 107, 127; Ken Regan (Camera 5), 145; United Press International,
endpapers, 21, 29, 32–33, 35, 44, 47, 52, 55, 58, 61, 72–73, 84, 89, 90, 99, 101, 113,
122, 126, 130, 135, 140; Wide World Photos, 22, 26, 69, 114, 143.

Cover photo by Focus On Sports

*To **Dad,***
Mom, and Sally
Charter Members of my Unsung Hero Hall of Fame

ACKNOWLEDGMENTS

The author would like to thank the following for their help in making the accomplishments of these unsung heroes better known: Bill Madden of United Press International; Jim Benagh; Woody Brandt; Baseball—Office of the Commissioner; the Public Relations Directors of the Major League clubs; and the writers and editors who contributed to the wealth of material contained in *The Sporting News* and *Sport* magazine.

Thanks also to Minnie Minoso, Nellie Fox, Luis Aparicio, Billy Pierce, and Jungle Jim Rivera, the unsung heroes of my youth, whose inspiring example had more to do with this book than they will ever know.

CONTENTS

INTRODUCTION   9

JOE RUDI   11

DOUG RADER   24

PHIL NIEKRO   38

THURMAN MUNSON   51

COOKIE ROJAS   63

BILLY WILLIAMS   77

MIKE CUELLAR   92

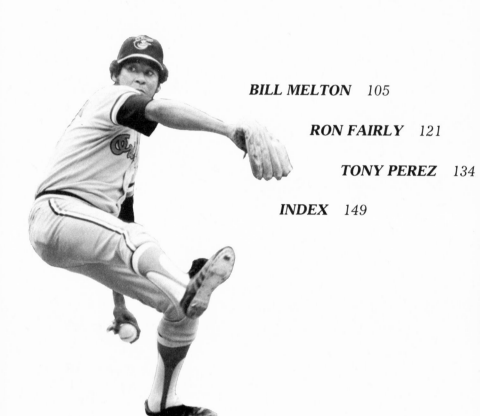

BILL MELTON   *105*

RON FAIRLY   *121*

TONY PEREZ   *134*

INDEX   *149*

INTRODUCTION

The ten major leaguers in this book include pitchers, outfielders, infielders, and a catcher. Some are great hitters, while others excel at defense. Some are just beginning their careers; others may soon be retiring. Yet there are two things they all have in common. Each man has made major contributions to the game of baseball—and each has failed to receive the kind of attention his fine play deserves.

The clutch hitting of Oakland's Joe Rudi and Cincinnati's Tony Perez helped their teams to World Series victories. Super-slugger Bill Melton was an American League home-run champion, and Billy Williams won the National League's batting title. Pitching aces Phil Niekro and Mike Cuellar were both 20-game winners. And all-star defensemen Thurman Munson, Cookie Rojas, Doug Rader, and Ron Fairly were invaluable in the field. Yet despite their great achievements, for one reason or another these stars were often underrated.

Although these players were never fully appreciated by the fans and sportswriters, their teammates and managers certainly knew their worth. Baseball is a team sport, and it takes at least nine men to win a game. While a few superstars may get most of the headlines, it is the unsung heroes who are often the heart of a team. The players spotlighted here are just a handful of the many pros who do their jobs with little fanfare. Perhaps in a future book other unsung heroes will also receive some long-overdue recognition.

JOE RUDI

From their flashy green and gold uniforms to their long shaggy haircuts and bushy mustaches, the Oakland A's were baseball's most colorful team. They were also the best. During the early 1970s the A's completely dominated the game, winning three world championships in a row.

The Oakland line-up glittered with stars. Outfielder Reggie Jackson was a consistent long-ball threat and winner of the Most Valuable Player award in 1973. Team captain and third baseman Sal Bando was known for his clutch hitting. Bert Campaneris was one of the swiftest and best-fielding shortstops in the game. And before he signed his multi-million-dollar contract with the New York Yankees in 1975, pitcher Jim "Catfish" Hunter was the brightest star of all.

And then there was Joe Rudi. Unlike his Oakland teammates, Joe didn't really excel at any one specialty—but there was nothing he couldn't do. Primarily a high-percentage batter, he could hit for power, too. He could apply the hit-and-run and bunt as well as anyone. He could steal a base with ease, and he got more than his share of walks. And to top it off, he was one of the best defensive outfielders in the majors.

Joe was different from his teammates off the field, too. While the others publicly criticized the Oakland management and made headlines with their frequent locker room fights, Joe stayed out of the limelight. "I've always been a fairly easygoing guy," he explained. "I just try to keep my mouth shut, do my job, and keep out of people's way."

Joe's low-keyed personality may have kept his name out of the newspapers and magazines, but the men who played with him were well aware of his value to the team.

"I'll tell you about Joe Rudi," Reggie Jackson said. "Nicest guy in the league—underrated, underpaid, a self-made ballplayer, and the best left fielder in the American League."

Oakland captain Sal Bando echoed Jackson's remarks. "You don't win pennants without a guy like that," he said. "You need me and Jackson to drive in runs. You need a guy like Catfish Hunter to pitch. But you need a guy like Rudi to drive in runs, get on base, and do some of the big and little

Oakland's Joe Rudi heads for first base after drawing a walk.

things before the big guys get up there. To me, he's a hundred-thousand-dollar ballplayer. If I'm a hundred-thousand-dollar ballplayer, so is he. I wouldn't trade him for anybody."

And as one-time Oakland manager Dick Williams said, "I'd take twenty-five Joe Rudis. I'm sure one of them would be able to pitch."

Joseph Oden Rudi learned to play baseball in Modesto, California, where he was born on September 7, 1946. "It was a constant battle between me and my father about playing ball," Joe recalled. "He was from the old country, Norway, and that just wasn't part of that culture. He thought I should be doing homework or something constructive."

Fortunately, Joe got lots of encouragement from his coach at Downey High School, Jerry Streeter, a former minor leaguer. Streeter first used Joe at shortstop because he felt Rudi's defensive talents would be wasted in the outfield. However, Streeter correctly predicted that the 6-foot-2, 215-pound youngster might eventually wind up in the outfield because of his size.

Baseball was only one of Rudi's activities in high school. He was a fine wrestler and starred on the football team, playing cornerback on defense and split end on offense. Rudi seriously considered playing football in college, but he soon had second thoughts about his future.

"I really loved football," Joe explained. "But I

14

saw that in college there would be guys weighing a hundred pounds more than I would, so I forgot about it.''

Football's loss was baseball's gain. While he was still in high school, Joe drew the attention of several major league clubs. But then he suffered an injury, and most of them lost interest. One scout who did stick with him was Don Pries of the Kansas City Athletics. And in 1964 (before they moved to Oakland) Joe signed with the A's.

Rudi's first two years of pro ball were spent in the low minors, where he batted a consistent but unimpressive .252 and .254. The breakthrough came in Joe's third campaign (1966). It was a big year in more ways than one. For starters, Joe was assigned to play right at home, in Modesto. It was there that his parents first saw him play. And before too long, they were both avid fans. Playing with future A's teammates like Reggie Jackson and Dave Duncan on the California League's Class A team, Rudi had a super season. He hit .297, slugged 24 homers, and drove in 85 runs. To top it off, he took advantage of being so close to home by marrying his high school sweetheart.

In 1967 Joe was promoted to the A's farm club in Birmingham of the Southern League. This time one of his teammates was Rollie Fingers, another future member of the world champion A's. Rudi had his second standout year in a row, finishing the season with a .288 batting average, 13 home runs, and 70 RBI's. During that same season Joe

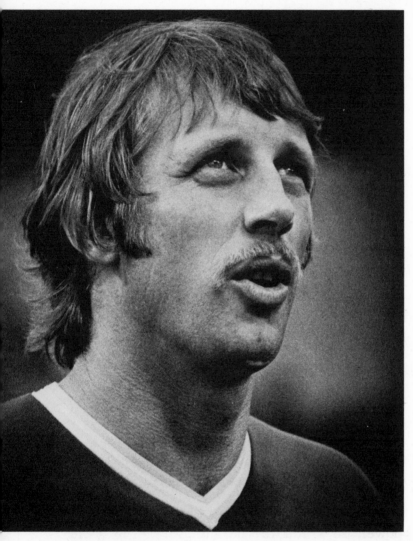

Joe Rudi: "I just try to keep my mouth shut, do my job, and keep out of people's way."

got his first crack at the majors, playing in 19 games with the A's.

At the start of 1968 the A's moved to Oakland and Rudi moved back to the minors—this time to Vancouver. After batting .317 in his first 16 games, Joe was again called up to the majors. But he wasn't very impressive in 68 games for Oakland that summer.

Joe began the 1969 season with the A's farm club in Iowa. As usual, he got off to a red-hot start, racking up a .354 average, 11 home runs, and 65 RBI's in 57 games. Again he was brought up to Oakland, and again he had trouble hitting against big league pitching.

Then in 1970 Oakland hired a new hitting coach, former major league catcher Charley Lau, and Joe took a giant step forward. Before long, there wasn't a pitcher in the game who could intimidate Joe Rudi.

"I was a pull hitter when I first came up," Rudi explained. "I held the bat high like Yaz [Boston slugger Carl Yastrzemski] and I took a big swing. Charley Lau changed me around. He closed up my stance and taught me a more compact, quicker swing. I learned to go with the pitch. I'm the type of player who has to concentrate on being consistent, doing all things well. I had some talent, but nowhere near what Reggie [Jackson] had. I could never run and throw with him or hit with such power, so I had to learn to do well in other things."

17

The 1970 season was Rudi's first full summer in the major leagues, and with the help of Lau his hitting got better and better. Using his new and somewhat unorthodox stance, Joe batted .309 with 11 home runs and 42 RBI's in 106 major league games. The following year, 1971, his average dipped to .267 with 10 homers and 52 RBI's in 127 games. Although his offensive statistics were not very impressive, he continued to excel in left field, leading all American League outfielders in defense.

That season the A's gave their first real indication of championship potential. They won the American League Western Division title—the first crown of any kind for the A's in Oakland—but were outclassed by Baltimore in the playoffs.

The 1972 season was Joe's first as a full-time starter in the A's outfield. And, not so coincidentally, it was the A's first year as world champions. Playing in 147 games, Rudi hit .305 with 19 home runs, 75 RBI's, and 94 runs scored. He led the league in hits, tied for the top in triples, was second in runs and doubles, third in total bases, fifth in batting average, and sixth in slugging percentage. His defense was as good as ever, and he played left field in his All-Star game debut.

Joe played a big part in Oakland's successful bid for the American League pennant, but it was in the World Series against the Cincinnati Reds that he really starred.

Oakland won the Series opener, and in game

two Joe hit a homer in the third inning to give the A's an early lead. The A's were leading 2–0 when the Reds came to bat in the bottom of the ninth inning. The first man up made it safely to first base. Then Cincinnati third baseman Denis Menke came to the plate. Menke swung and hit a long drive deep to left field. It looked like a sure home run. But Joe raced back to the wall, leaped up, and made a spectacular grab to rob the Reds of the potential tying run. Many experts consider that catch to be one of the greatest defensive plays in Series history.

The Reds eventually scored a run, but the A's hung on to win 2–1. Rudi's great catch in the outfield and his third-inning homer had been the deciding factors in Oakland's victory. Although Cincinnati came back and stretched the classic to seven games, the A's went on to win their first world championship.

Joe's contributions were soon forgotten, however. By the time the Series was over, Oakland catcher Gene Tenace was getting all the attention. He socked four home runs that autumn, tying a Series record—and receiving the hero's laurels.

The A's repeated as world champs in 1973. And even though he missed over 20 games because of an injury, Joe had another solid season. He batted .270 with 12 home runs and 66 RBI's. But Rudi's worth couldn't be measured by statistics alone, as he clearly demonstrated during the '73 playoffs and World Series.

In the playoff series against Baltimore, for example, Joe batted an unimpressive .222. Nevertheless, he was a dominant figure. He broke a 1–1 tie in the sixth inning of the second game with a home run. In the eighth inning of game three he singled in the tying run to send the game into extra innings, and the A's went on to win. And in the pivotal fifth and deciding game he drove in the game-winning run.

In the World Series against the New York Mets, Joe continued to shine. He had the game-winning hit in the opener, drove the tying run home in the third game, and scored the winning run in the finale. He compiled a .333 batting average and tied a Series record for most chances and putouts (7) in left field for one game.

In 1974 Joe's regular-season statistics finally reflected his true abilities. Playing in more games than ever before (158), he led the A's in batting average (.293), hits (174), and doubles (39). He tied for third in homers with Bando (22) and was second to Jackson in RBI's (99). He also led the league in total bases and doubles and took third place in the RBI department. As usual, he was superb in the field.

The A's had an equally successful year, winning yet another world championship. Rudi was at his best in the '74 Series against the L.A. Dodgers. He averaged over .300 at the plate and led all hitters in RBI's. In the fourth game he set up the winning runs with a sacrifice bunt. And his seventh-inning

During game two of the 1972 World Series, Rudi makes a spectacular catch to rob Cincinnati of the game-tying run.

Attempting to steal second in the 1973 Series, Joe crashes into Met Felix Millan (16), who makes the tag.

home run was the crowning blow in the fifth and final game.

Joe was moved to first base in 1975, and he continued to shine at the plate. The A's took a comfortable lead in the American League West.

22

But early in August Joe tore some ligaments in his left thumb and was put on the disabled list. Kansas City, the second-place team in the West, began making a bid for the division crown.

Hearing the news about Rudi's injury, his ex-teammate Catfish Hunter predicted: "Without Rudi, the A's are gonna know that they're in some ballgames in September."

The A's hung on to win the division title, and Rudi was back in the line-up for the American League playoffs. But it was clear that Joe still wasn't quite up to par when the A's faced the Boston Red Sox for the pennant. His teammates were clearly having problems too, for the three-time world champions bowed to the Sox in three straight games.

Fans and experts came up with a variety of explanations for Oakland's surprising defeat. But that was already in the past. Looking towards the future, most agreed that with a healthy Rudi back in '76, the A's might well begin another string of championships.

DOUG RADER

On April 9, 1974, the San Diego Padres were defeated 9–5 by the Houston Astros. It was San Diego's fourth game—and fourth loss—of the season. In their three previous games, they had been on the short end of 8–0, 8–0, and 9–2 scores. The 39,083 fans in the San Diego Stadium were thoroughly disgusted with their team. But no one was more upset than Ray Kroc, owner of the Padres and principal shareholder of the McDonald's hamburger chain.

Kroc didn't wait to get to the locker room to scold his players. In the middle of the eighth inning he picked up the public address microphone and told them—and the thousand of fans still in their seats—just what he thought of their latest game. Kroc accused the team of lacking hustle and of not giving the fans their money's worth. He made it clear that he would no longer stand for such lackadaisical play and threatened to make some changes unless his players shaped up fast.

Like everyone else in the ballpark, the Houston Astros could hardly believe their ears. The arena buzzed with comments about Kroc's outburst. Running true to form, Astro team captain and third baseman Doug Rader came up with the most controversial remark. Referring to Kroc's connection with McDonald's, Rader quipped to the press: "Who does he think he's dealing with—a bunch of short-order cooks?"

While the outspoken Rader never meant to demean anyone's occupation, outraged short-order cooks all over the country demanded an apology. The next time Rader and the Astros arrived in San Diego, they were welcomed by "Short-Order Cooks' Night." Some 1,323 cooks joined the rest of the crowd in San Diego Stadium, determined to make Rader eat his words.

But Rader took the awkward situation in stride. When the fun-loving team captain brought the starting line-up out to home plate, he was wearing a chef's hat and apron and carrying a frying pan. The crowd cheered his sportsmanship.

"I think he was really a good sport going out there like that," said one short-order cook. "I think the man is great," said another.

Although Rader hadn't planned it, his coopera-

Doug Rader, Houston's high-flying third baseman, plays leapfrog with Cesar Cedeno and Bob Watson during spring training.

tion with his hosts continued. That night he played one of his worst games ever, making one error, striking out twice, and flying out to end the game with the bases loaded. To the delight of the San Diego fans, Houston lost 5–4. But even that didn't dampen Rader's high spirits. "I didn't have much of a night," he said after the game, "but at least I pleased the cooks."

Known affectionately as the "Red Rooster," Rader was baseball's best-known practical joker and stand-up comic. Teammates, friends, and fans were all fair game for Rader's pranks.

A classic example of Rader's unusual sense of humor was broadcast on national television. Sportscaster Jim Bouton asked him to give some advice to little leaguers. "I've always thought they should not only chew the gum that comes with the baseball cards, but they should also eat the cards," was Rader's deadpan reply. "Only the cards of the good ballplayers," he added. "Bad statistics can't be properly digested."

Because his off-the-field antics often made headlines on the sports pages, many fans failed to take Rader seriously as a player. But in any game situation, he was a true professional. "He's the best third baseman in the National League," said Pete Rose.

In addition to his defense, which put him in a very select class of fielding third basemen, Rader was one of the game's most dependable clutch hitters. Whether it was a single in the ninth to tie a game, or a twelfth-inning home run to run to win it, Rader seemed to be there when it really counted.

Douglas Lee Rader was born July 30, 1944, in Chicago, Illinois. The adopted son of a commercial artist, he grew up in suburban Northbrook. Because his father had had his own football and soccer careers cut short by injuries, he forbade young Doug to play contact sports.

For a while Doug did avoid contact sports, but his father would hardly have approved of the activities his son chose instead. Doug ran around with what he called a "rough and rowdy" crowd that always seemed to be looking for trouble.

Eventually the sports bug got to Doug. At the age of 16, under the false name of Lou D'Bardini, he entered the Golden Gloves boxing tournament. The alias, of course, was to hide his activities from his father. Doug's boxing career was brief, however. It lasted less than one round!

In high school Rader stuck to baseball and basketball—with his father's blessings. He played well enough to receive an athletic scholarship to Illinois Wesleyan University.

Before long, Doug was up to his old tricks. Disregarding the most basic rule of amateur athletics, he signed a contract to play semi-pro hockey. Naturally he couldn't play under his real name. Just a few years before, he had used Lou D'Bardini to hide his boxing career from his

The camera catches Doug in an uncharacteristic mood in 1971. The dejected Astro had just been sidelined by a shoulder injury.

father. Now he set out to conceal his identity from Wesleyan by becoming Dominic Bulganzio the hockey player.

Although hockey had very few fans in that part of Illinois, Doug had always had great enthusiasm for the game. "Hockey was always my first love," he said. "But playing it in Illinois is like playing baseball in Germany."

Doug eventually quit the team—before his violation was discovered—and began to concentrate on baseball. While he was still at Wesleyan, major league scouts came to see him in droves. And in September 1964 he signed with the Houston Astros.

Rader began his professional career with the Astros' Class A team at Durham, North Carolina, in 1965. He got off to a fast start and was soon leading the Carolina League in hitting. But that didn't last long. Later in the season the highly competitive Rader pounded his fist against the wall in a fit of temper and hurt his hand. He suffered in silence for the rest of the season because he was afraid to tell his manager about the injury. Not surprisingly, he ended his first pro season with a disappointing .209 average, 14 homers, and 38 RBI's.

Despite his late-season slump, Doug had impressed the Astros. The following year he advanced to the AA Amarillo club in the Texas League, where he continued to improve. He finished his second minor league season with a .290 batting average, 16 home runs, and 74 runs batted in.

Doug was also fielding superbly and contributing in other little ways. Perhaps the most impressive thing about his game was his hustle. He played the game with 100 percent effort. "I like the aggressive part of baseball," Doug said, some-what understating his love of competition.

Rader's fine season in Amarillo did not go unnoticed in Houston. Newcomers to the league, the Astros had been formed in the 1962 expansion. Now they were still struggling to reach respectability. They kept a sharp eye on their farm clubs, in hopes of finding players of major league caliber. The aggressive Rader, with his skill both at bat and in the field, was just the man they were looking for.

Rader started the 1967 season at the Astros' top farm club in Oklahoma City—and finished it in Houston. Because of an injury sustained while serving his army reserve obligation, he had trouble throwing. Therefore, he made his big league debut at first base. In 47 games with the Astros he hit .333 with 2 home runs, 10 doubles, and 26 RBI's.

Rader was not his usual happy-go-lucky self during the early part of the 1968 campaign. Doug was ready to pick up where he'd left off the previous season, but manager Grady Hatton had other plans for him. Hatton benched Rader and told him to watch veteran third baseman Bob Aspromonte for a while. The impatient rookie had no choice but to sit and wait. At one point Doug was so frustrated that he went up to Aspromonte and predicted that he, Rader, would get the veteran's job.

In June of that '68 season, manager Hatton was

Rader dives back to first base after attempting to steal second in a 1969 game against the St. Louis Cardinals.

fired and replaced by Harry Walker. Walker was pleased with Rader's obvious desire to play and decided to give the young third baseman a chance to show what he could do. Doug's prediction came true at the end of the season when Aspromonte was traded to Atlanta. The following year Rader was Houston's starting third baseman. Playing in 155 games, he socked 11 homers and drove in 83 runs.

In 1970 Doug's batting average was an unimpressive .252, but he was among the National League leaders in both home runs (25) and RBI's (87). To top it off, he won the Gold Glove award as the league's top defensive third baseman.

Doug's totals dipped just a bit in '71, but for the next three seasons he was a model of consistency. His '72 statistics included 22 homers and 90 RBI's. In 1973 he had 21 home runs and 89 RBI's, and the following year he belted 17 homers and drove in 78 runs. And each year he won the Gold Glove award for his fielding.

During those years Doug's batting average never went above .257. But fortunately, the Astros realized that good hitting can sometimes be a matter of quality, not quantity. Doug got his hits when they counted most—usually with men on base.

"The only thing I think about is runs batted in," Rader once said. "My job is to drive in runs and do a good job at third base. If I do this, I'm earning my money."

A powerful home-run hitter, Rader is about to send one out of the ballpark.

As his RBI totals clearly showed, Rader more than earned his money. In one week during the 1973 season he slammed three 3-run homers. Later that season Doug suffered through an awful hitting slump, going to bat more than 20 times without a single base hit. When he finally came out of his slump, he did it in typical Rader style—with a grand-slam home run against the New York Mets.

Doug had a disappointing season in 1975, with only 12 home runs and 48 RBI's. Yet even then he still came through when his team needed him most. On May 14, for instance, the Astros were mired in the cellar after a long losing streak. Another defeat seemed inevitable as they faced the Chicago Cubs, who were then in first place in the National League West. But Rader had had enough of losing. That day he hit one homer and then another, driving in a total of five runs to give the Astros a much-needed victory.

As dangerous as Rader could be at the plate, most experts agreed that his real talent was in the field. Unfortunately, not much notice is given to defensive play, so Doug's skill at third base was often ignored. Many experts, however, have compared his glove to that of superstar Brooks Robinson of Baltimore.

"Going by what I've seen on television, I'd probably have to say Robinson is the best," Rader said. "But he had all the chances. You have to be out there to be great, and he has played in lots of World Series."

Rader and the Astros rarely made it to the first division—much less to the Series. Although the Astros were loaded with such great talent as Cesar Cedeno, Lee May, Bob Watson, Tommy Helms, and Rader himself, they never got into the "big" games and were seldom seen by a national audience. After the '75 season, Doug was traded to the San Diego Padres, another non-contending team. Had Rader played with a winning team like Baltimore, he would surely have received more recognition.

But as things turned out, Rader became baseball's most famous practical joker and perhaps least publicized third baseman. His practical jokes may have overshadowed his professional abilities and earned him a reputation as a flake instead of a superstar, but Doug had no complaints.

"I don't think it's hurt me," said Rader. "People realize the fun I have is harmless. And it doesn't take anything away from how I play the game. Sure I do a lot of joking around, but it's like a defense mechanism to counteract the seriousness of the game. It takes the pressure off. The only time I fool around is when I'm off the field."

And as his National League opponents would be the first to admit, when he was on the field, Douglas Lee Rader was all business.

PHIL NIEKRO

In 1959 the Milwaukee Braves signed a young pitcher named Phil Niekro for $500. Even in those days, $500 wasn't much of a bonus—but then Niekro wasn't much of a pitcher. "I was just a skinny kid who couldn't throw hard enough to break a mirror," Phil admitted.

Fortunately, Niekro didn't have to rely solely on his strength. He had a special "soft" pitch, the knuckleball, that was just as effective as any fastball. Phil's knuckler came off his fingertips with almost no spin. It seemed to sail to the plate. Then, just before it reached the batter, it would break—dipping, bobbing, floating. It was an unpredictable, tricky pitch, and even the most consistent hitters had trouble with it.

For more than a decade, Phil and his knuckleball baffled National League sluggers. By the end

Atlanta ace Phil Niekro gets set to hurl his famous knuckleball during a 1975 game.

of 1975 Niekro had two seasons with 20 or more wins to his credit, a career total of 145 victories, 2,494 innings pitched, and a fine 2.94 earned run average.

Unfortunately, not too many fans were aware of Phil's excellent statistics. For a number of years (first in Milwaukee and then in Atlanta) he was the only real standout on the Braves pitching staff. While the experts criticized the Braves' overall weak pitching, they rarely mentioned Niekro as the single exception.

The problem took an unusual turn in 1974. The Braves' pitchers improved greatly that year. In fact, they became one of the best staffs in the league. Sportswriters finally began covering the Braves' hurlers, but now it was the youngsters— men like Buzz Capra—who made the news. Niekro suddenly had the bad luck of being the unsung "old timer" on an exciting new staff.

Phil Niekro was born April 1, 1939, in Blaine, Ohio. His father was a big baseball fan, who had once hoped to become a big leaguer himself. Phil and his younger brother Joe greatly benefited from their dad's interest.

Mr. Niekro was a coal miner. "Every day he'd come home from work with black soot all over him," Phil recalled. "We'd wait until he put his lunch pail down, and then we'd go at it, playing catch in the back yard for hours."

One day Phil's father taught him a pitch he'd thrown as a young player. "I was fascinated," Phil remembered. "He showed me how to hold it. From that day on, we'd have a contest to see who could make it spin the least. Finally I got to throwing it so good that Dad just quit playing." That pitch, of course, was the knuckleball, and Phil's dad (like most catchers) found a good knuckleball difficult and dangerous to catch.

Phil used his knuckler to lead his Bridgeport, Ohio, high school team to one victory after another. Phil suffered only one defeat in his whole high school career. In that game he was tagged for a home run in a 1–0 loss. (That homer was hit by Bill Mazeroski, who later became a star with the Pittsburgh Pirates.)

Phil wasn't the only great athlete playing baseball for Bridgeport. His teammate John Havlicek went on to become one of pro basketball's superstars. Phil and John were great friends and lived on the same street.

"We played all three sports together in high school [baseball, basketball, and football] at one time or another," Havlicek recalled. "Phil was a pretty good basketball player and had a good outside shot.

"In baseball, our catcher back in high school used to have nightmares the night before the game he knew Niekro would pitch. He spent a lot of time diving and running back to the screen after those knucklers. But eventually he got pretty good at catching them."

Surprisingly, the people of Bridgeport weren't overly impressed by their hometown baseball and basketball stars. Football was their game. "You know," Phil said, "our class is probably better known in Bridgeport as the first team to beat our arch-rival Martins Ferry in football in 27 years."

On the basis of his great high school credentials, Phil hoped to have a chance to play pro ball after graduation. But he didn't get a single offer from the big league scouts. In those days the knuckler was considered a "freak" pitch.

Phil finally got a chance to show what he could do when the Milwaukee Braves conducted an open tryout camp in a nearby town. The Braves weren't exactly overwhelmed by Niekro, but they were interested enough to sign him on as a pitcher–first baseman.

Phil began his professional career in 1959 in the New York–Pennsylvania League at Wellsville. He spent the next five years in such minor league towns as McCook, Nebraska; Jacksonville, Florida; Austin, Texas; Louisville, Kentucky; and Denver, Colorado. After one year in the minors he whittled his earned run average from 7.46 down to 3.12. The Braves were impressed with his progress but felt he still had a lot to learn. During the next three seasons Phil was fairly consistent, and his ERA ranged between 2.77 and 3.86.

"Those were the years when I could have become discouraged," Phil admitted. "I always felt I could pitch in the majors, but I kept shuttling back and forth. I ran into a lot of people who told me I was too young to throw the knuckleball, that I should drop it. But there were also a lot of people who said I had a great pitch and that I should stick with it.

"For a couple of years I didn't know what to do. Then I finally decided that I couldn't throw hard enough to make it any other way. The only way I could make it would be as a knuckleball pitcher."

Phil's decision to stick with the knuckler turned out to be a good one. In 1964, after a brief time out for military service, he was promoted to the Braves' AAA club at Denver. He compiled a fine 11-5 mark there and was called up to the big club at the end of the season.

Phil spent all of 1965 in Milwaukee, but he didn't see too much action that year. When Phil first hit the majors, he was automatically assigned a relief role. At the time, baseball's most successful knuckleballers were Hoyt Wilhelm and Eddie Fisher—both relievers. The Braves naturally assumed that Niekro, too, would be most effective coming out of the bullpen.

In his rookie season Phil was credited with two wins, three losses, and a fine 2.88 ERA. The following year, the Braves moved to Atlanta. Phil compiled a 4-3 record in 28 games there before he

Niekro throws the first pitch of the 1969 National League playoffs to New York Met Tommy Agee.

was sent down to Richmond for some more seasoning.

In 1967 Phil was back in the majors—this time for good. That season several Braves pitchers were injured, so Phil was finally put into the starting rotation. In his very first start he hurled a two-hit shutout against Philadelphia.

"I think they always had the idea that I didn't have enough stamina to go nine innings," Phil said. "I think I opened up a few eyes."

Phil was throwing the knuckler better than ever, but unfortunately his catchers were having a rough time holding on to it. In one game he came in as a reliever with the score tied in the ninth inning. Phil struck the batter out with his knuckler, but the catcher bobbled the ball on the third strike. The batter made it to first base, and the catcher was charged with a passed ball. To make things worse, the runner advanced to second base on another passed ball. The next man up sent the runner home, and the Braves lost the game.

Still, Phil finished the season with a winning 11–9 record and led all National League pitchers with an excellent 1.87 ERA. He followed that up in 1968 with a 14–12 record and an earned run average of 2.59.

Then came 1969—a season of firsts. Phil was named to his first All-Star team and went on to his first 20-victory year. He won 23 games, compiled a 2.57 ERA, and hurled an impressive 284 innings. To top it all off, the Braves won the division title in the National League West—their first title of any kind in Atlanta. They were favored to win the National League playoffs but were upset by the New York Mets in three straight games.

Phil had an off year in 1970. "That was my own fault," he admitted. "I figured I had my knuckleball down pat and spent all spring training working on my slider. Then, when the season began, I found that I couldn't control my knuckleball as I did the year before. I began to lose confidence. That's when I made up my mind that if I wanted to stay in the big league, I'd have to concentrate on my knuckleball."

Niekro came back in 1971 and '72 with 15 and 16 wins, respectively, and continued his "Iron Man" role with 269 and 282 innings pitched. He was truly the stopper of the staff.

The 1973 season was more of the same—until August 5, when Niekro pitched his greatest game ever. That day Phil Niekro etched his name in the record books by hurling his first no-hitter. His 9–0 rout of the San Diego Padres was the first and only no-hitter in the National League that year and the first ever in Atlanta Stadium.

After the last pitch was thrown, catcher Phil Casanova leaped up and hugged Niekro. When asked about his display of emotion, Casanova replied, "I had to. He's a beautiful guy."

"I never had a no-hitter, except in a sandlot game," said the triumphant knuckleballer. "I was aware I had one going, but I wouldn't even look at

46

Phil celebrates his 1973 no-hitter with his jubilant teammates.

the scoreboard. And nobody else on the bench said anything to me."

Then Phil dedicated the game to his father, who was ill in a hospital. "Maybe this will perk him up," he said.

Niekro's great moment was one bright spot in a long disappointing season for the Braves. They finished with a dismal 76–85 record. The problem was clearly their pitching. With the exception of Niekro, Atlanta's starting staff was nothing to rave about, but its bullpen was even weaker. Before the '74 season began, the Braves considered using Niekro as a full-time reliever to give the staff more depth.

"If moving to the bullpen will help get us closer to first place, then I'm for it," Niekro said. "I still prefer to start. But I came up as a relief man, and if I'm more help to the club this way, then I'll be in the bullpen."

The rearrangement never came about. In 1974 Niekro and newcomer Buzz Capra led the best Braves pitching staff since Warren Spahn and Lew Burdette hurled them to the top during the late 1950s.

Although Phil had once vowed never to stop concentrating on his knuckler, that season he added some other good pitches to his repertoire. "I still am throwing mainly knuckleballs, but I've developed a screwball and improved my slider," he explained. "I'd been fooling around with it on the side for about three or four years. Finally I decided it was good enough to use in the game. Fortunately, it worked out well for me. I became convinced I should try it when I looked around and saw how successful the other pitchers were. I still throw the knuckler eighty to eighty-five percent of the time, but the screwball gives the hitters something else to look for."

Phil kept the opposing batters guessing throughout '74. He picked up his 20th victory on the very last day of the season and finished with a 2.38 ERA. He also set Atlanta records for most strike-outs (195) and shutouts (6) in a season. In addition, he led the league in total innings pitched (302) and complete games (18) and compiled a perfect fielding record in 64 chances.

"I was surprised I could win twenty," Phil said at the end of the season. "I never thought about it too much because it didn't look as if I'd do it. Then, all of a sudden there it was.

"Every pitcher tries for twenty wins each season. That's a standard goal. But nothing pleases me more than those 300 innings pitched."

The Braves just about reversed their '73 finish to a winning 88–74 record. Niekro should have been the hero of the year. But Capra, who had a 16–8 record and a league-leading 2.28 ERA in his first year as a Brave, stole the show.

Compared to Capra, Niekro was a real old-timer. But compared to the most famous knuckle-baller of all time—Hoyt Wilhelm—he was just a kid. Wilhelm had pitched for 21 years before retiring at the age of 49. Niekro didn't know if he could last as long as Wilhelm. But at the age of 36, after completing his first decade in the majors, Phil was still looking toward the future.

"The first ten years were my toughest," he said in 1975. "I figure my next ten will be easier. Not that I'll let up when I'm pitching. It is just that I think the things I have learned will make my job easier."

THURMAN MUNSON

Because of his stocky build, his teammates affectionately dubbed him "Squatty," "Round Man," or "Turtle." And Yankee super-catcher Thurman Munson was the first to admit that he just wasn't a glamor player.

"I'm little; I'm pudgy," he said. "I don't look good doing things. Those big guys look superb."

By "big guys," Munson undoubtably meant Cincinnati's Johnny Bench and Boston's Carlton Fisk, two other fine catchers who seemed to get the lion's share of publicity, while Munson was rarely credited for his outstanding work.

"I guess the press doesn't like me," Munson once said. "It used to bother me, but I don't think about it anymore. Anyway, I'd rather *play* baseball than talk about it."

Yankee catcher Thurman Munson was as valuable at the plate as he was behind it. Here he takes a big swing during a 1975 game.

Fortunately, in Munson's case, actions spoke louder than words. In his first six full seasons in the majors, he averaged over .300 three different times. He was named Rookie of the Year in 1970 and was a perennial member of the All-Star team.

While his offensive game alone could have given Munson the edge over most catchers, it was his defense that was really spectacular. When it came to gunning down a potential base-stealer, no one was quicker than Munson. And when it came to handling a wild pitch, no one was surer.

Of course, New York fans had very high standards for their catchers. Such all-time greats as Bill Dickey, Yogi Berra, and Elston Howard had all spent their greatest years behind home plate in Yankee Stadium. Munson had a lot to live up to.

Thurman Munson was born in Akron, Ohio, on June 7, 1947, only a year after Yogi Berra made the majors with the Yankees. He grew up in nearby Canton, where his father was a truck driver. Mr. Munson earned just enough money to make ends meet for Thurman and his three brothers and sisters.

"We had food and clothing," Thurman recalled. "But not a dime left over."

Despite the lack of luxuries, Thurman had a happy childhood. Encouraged by his dad, he began playing sports early. In high school Thurman was an all-round athlete. He did double duty on the football field, playing linebacker on defense and wingback on offense. He also starred on the basketball court, where he averaged 20 points per game and was selected to the All-County team. But his number one sport was always baseball.

In high school Munson played the infield except for one brief stint behind the plate. "I started to catch only because we had a pitcher, Jerome Pruett, with a blazing fastball and no one else could hold him," Munson explained. "I caught him in four games, but I really didn't start catching until my sophomore year in college."

Munson was a natural for the catcher's slot, a position where quickness is the key. "Anything done with the hands always has come easy for me," he said. "As a kid, I was always using my hands. I guess that helped my quickness.

"I remember playing some forty games of ping-pong many nights, which certainly helped develop my dexterity. I would play with my brother, my dad, or by myself if no one was around."

Munson turned down a flock of college football scholarships to attend Kent State University in Ohio on a baseball scholarship. There he developed into a fine catcher, using his great hands and overall natural ability to win All-America honors. Right after his junior year, Munson signed with the Yankees.

Yankee scout Gene Woodling (a former major league star) had been greatly impressed with Thurman's college performances. "I saw him in five games, and that was all I needed," said

An angry Munson leaps straight up in the air in a dispute with the home plate ump.

Woodling. "He didn't look like an athlete, yet he proved he was outstanding as soon as the game started. His speed, throwing, and catching were eye-catching."

In his first minor league season (1968) Thurman was even more impressive. Playing at Binghamton in the Eastern League (Class AA), he hit .301 in 71 games. In '69 Munson took time off for military duty, but played 28 games for Syracuse (AAA) and hit .363. At the end of the season he was called up to New York and played 26 games with the Yankees.

"I never worried about making the majors," Munson said. "I just didn't think it would happen as fast as it did."

In one of his first major league games, Munson gave a hint of things to come. The Yankees were leading the Cleveland Indians by two runs. But in the bottom of the ninth inning the Indians got a man on first base. The next man up, slugger Ken Harrelson, posed a big threat at the plate—the potential tying run. Before Harrelson had a chance to break up the game, Munson fired the ball to first base and picked off the runner by a mile.

"They haven't seen that play around the Yankees in a long time," said Harrelson on his way back to the dugout after the game.

Things weren't always so easy for Munson, however. His official rookie year (1970) got off to a disappointing start. "I had never been in a slump before, and I didn't know what was happening," Thurman recalled. "It was tough going to my room at night and having that on my mind. But I didn't know whether to worry or not.

"Then Ralph Houk [the Yankee manager] told me I'd be the regular catcher all year. It gave me more confidence. I kept plugging. There was no sense getting excited. I knew I could hit, and it was only a matter of time."

Munson bounced back as the season progressed. He did an excellent job behind the plate —and regained his touch in the batter's box. He wound up with a .302 batting average and won the Rookie of the Year award.

Munson didn't let his quick success go to his head. "I know I still have a long way to go," he said. "I'm no superstar, nothing like that. A superstar is a guy who does it year after year. I've just done it for one year. I have a long way to go. There's a long road ahead of me."

Munson had another good year in 1971 and made his first appearance at an All-Star game. During the season Houk discussed Thurman's future. "I'd be very satisfied if Munson has the same kind of year this year that he had in 1970. But the great thing about him is that as good as he was last year, he is going to get better. And better. There is no telling how much better he can get."

That season Thurman's defense was almost perfect. He led all major league catchers in fielding with a .998 mark and committed just one error

**Thurman puts the tag on a sliding Frank Robinson during a 1971
Yankee-Oriole contest.**

in 615 chances (a Yankee record). The lone error occurred when he was knocked practically unconscious in a collision at home plate and dropped the ball.

The following year Munson batted .280 and continued his fine defensive play. Just as Houk had predicted, he was getting better and better. Thurman really reached star status in 1973. He maintained a .301 average and collected 20 homers, 29 doubles, and 74 RBI's. He played in his second All-Star game and won the Gold Glove award as the American League's top defensive catcher.

But Thurman's value to the Yankees couldn't be measured by mere statistics. In a game against Baltimore that year, he played one of his typically sound, though unflashy, games. It was the kind of game that never makes headlines but can mean the difference between a winning or losing season for a team.

Baltimore was in first place, and the Yanks had already lost the first game of a three-game series. They needed this one to even it out. In the top of the second inning, Munson singled up the middle against Baltimore ace Mike Cuellar. His next time at bat he singled again, this time to left field. The next batter up advanced him to second. Then the speedy Munson scored from second on a hard-hit single—when many players would have been held on third.

When Munson came to bat in the ninth, the

59

Yankees were down by two runs, but they had a man on first. Thurman connected with the ball and sent it soaring into the stands. He had tied up the game and given his team the momentum it needed to win in extra innings.

In 1974 Bill Virdon took over as manager, and the Yankees became contenders for the first time in years. But for Munson it was a totally frustrating season. With his throwing arm hurting badly, his defensive play suffered. He began to make errors, and opposing runners discovered it wasn't so hard to steal on him. As a result of the arm and a lingering sore thumb, his hitting suffered too.

To the competitive Munson, the season was pure torture. Still, he tried to think positively. "I keep telling myself things are going to change," he explained midway through the season. "And then I go three for four and feel great. And then I go nothing for eight and I'm derailed again. You can't say that I'm not blocking balls or hustling or helping the pitchers. When I pop up I just take off my helmet and put it on the rack and try next time. I'm trying as hard as I can."

A year like Munson went through in '74 either brings out the best or the worst in a person. In Munson's case, it showed his great attitude. "Even though he has had his problems," said manager Virdon, "he still helped us in a lot of ways—his defensive plays around the infield, tag plays, and calling games. All the pitchers want him to catch for them."

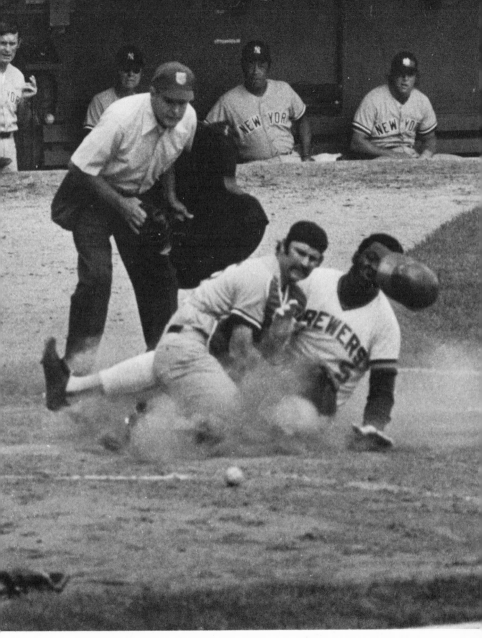

Milwaukee baserunner George Scott is safe at home when Munson loses the ball.

Munson finished the season with a .261 average and a low—for him—fielding percentage of .974. Even so, he drove in a creditable 60 runs and won the Gold Glove for the second year in a row. The Yankees just missed the playoffs, finishing two games behind the Eastern division champions. Virdon let it be known that with a healthy Munson, he was sure the Yankees would have won their first championship of any kind since 1964.

Thurman came back strong in 1975 and had his best season ever—a 3.18 batting average, 190 hits (third best in the league), 102 RBI's, and a .972 fielding percentage. But his contributions were lost in the excitement over the trades that brought Bobby Bonds and superstar Catfish Hunter to New York.

But Munson was still only 28 years old, and the way he was going he had many great years ahead of him. In time, perhaps, the fans and experts would come to see that Thurman Munson truly belonged in that exclusive Yankee catching club.

No matter what happened, though, Munson had no regrets about his career. "I love baseball," he said. "It's given me everything I have. Look, there are only about six hundred major leaguers in the country. You *have* to feel special."

COOKIE ROJAS

"He does it all," is just about the most complimentary phrase anyone can use to describe an athlete. In the case of a baseball player it would refer to someone who could hit, field, and run the bases with equal skill—someone like Cookie Rojas. But when people said that Rojas could do it all, they meant even more. In his long career, first with the Philadelphia Phillies and then the Kansas City Royals, Cookie literally did it all—playing all nine positions, including pitcher.

"The way it is in baseball," Rojas once said, "unless you have super ability, it is better to play more than one position. You have to do it. It is a way to stay in the major leagues."

Cookie played in minor league towns for six years before he won his first big league tryout—

and lost it after 39 unimpressive games. The next time he came up to the majors he was determined to stay for good. Because he was not a super-slugger, Cookie realized that he'd have to find another way to make himself valuable to his team. A fine second baseman, he worked hard on his fielding and eventually mastered several infield and outfield positions.

"Work, work, work! As long as I know Cookie, he is always working," said the late major leaguer Chico Ruiz.

"No matter how down you are or how tired you are, you gotta go out and play to win," Cookie explained. "That is the tag you want to get—the tag of a winner."

Although he never got the kind of acclaim that comes to baseball's great sluggers, Rojas did become a winner, contributing to his teams in countless ways.

Octavio Rivas Rojas, nicknamed "Cuqui" in Spanish and "Cookie" in English, was born in Havana, Cuba, on March 6, 1939. As a young boy he spent hours every day playing baseball in the streets of Havana and hours every night dreaming of becoming a major leaguer.

"I always wanted to be a ballplayer," Cookie said. "My father always wanted me to be a doctor."

To Cookie's delight and his father's dismay, Cookie signed with the Cincinnati Reds in 1956

Playing for Kansas City in 1973, the versatile Cookie Rojas lays down a bunt and takes off for first base.

when he was just 17 years old. "My father said I could try it for a year," he recalled. "If I didn't make it by then, I would go back to the books."

Cookie's first pro season was spent at West Palm Beach, Florida—and for a while it looked as if it might be his last. Without his great desire to play ball, he might have fallen by the wayside. Cookie faced all the usual problems of a young rookie—and more. Like the others, he had a lot to learn about the game and about living on his own. But he also had to learn a new language. At the time, Cookie spoke almost no English.

By the end of his first season, however, Cookie was hitting a respectable .275, had made the Florida State League All-Star team, and was adjusting well to his new life. When he returned to Havana for the winter, he was able to convince his father that he had a real future in the game.

"I told my father that baseball was a profession, too," Cookie said years later. "I told him I was serious about my profession. Now my father is proud that I'm a ballplayer."

In 1957 Rojas played in Wausau, Wisconsin, where he batted .262. He followed that up with a .254 average at Savannah, Georgia, in '58. It seemed unlikely that Cookie would ever develop into an exceptional hitter, but his excellent fielding and overall baseball savvy made up for his low batting average.

In 1959 Cookie got a chance to go home *and* further his baseball career at the same time. The

Reds' top farm team was then in Havana, and that's where he was assigned. But the excitement of playing in front of a hometown crowd was dimmed by the civil war that was going on in Cuba.

That year, Fidel Castro overthrew the government of Cuba and took charge himself. Many Cubans were happy about the change—the old government had been harsh and corrupt. But the change in government upset the lives of many others.

Playing in Havana in 1959, Cookie hit only .233. When Castro began forbidding ballplayers to travel to the United States (where the Havana club played all its away games), the league owners became nervous. Halfway through the 1960 season the Havana team was shifted to Jersey City, New Jersey. Cookie left Cuba knowing he might not be able to return even to visit his family as long as he played professional baseball. His performance in 1960 was no better than the previous year, and it began to look as if he would never reach the major leagues.

During the 1961 season, however, Cookie finally improved his batting, and in 1962 he was called up to Cincinnati. But again his excitement turned to disappointment. The 23-year-old infielder went to the Reds as a second baseman, but the team already had a fine second baseman, Don Blasingame, who was enjoying the greatest season of his life. Cookie was willing to try another position, but the Reds just weren't interested. When Cookie did get a chance to play, he did little to make them reconsider. After appearing in only 39 games, he was sent back to the minors.

Cookie's big break came in '63 after he was traded to the Philadelphia Phillies for pitcher Jim Owens. Although Cookie had a reputation for being a good-field, no-hit second baseman, Phillie manager Gene Mauch was impressed by the fact that he had played a number of positions in the minor leagues. Rojas played in only 64 games that season, but the following year he really came into his own. Manager Mauch took advantage of Cookie's versatility in the field by playing the youngster at seven different positions.

During one 1964 game against Cincinnati, Philadelphia's regular catcher, Gus Triandos, was injured. Then in the top of the ninth, back-up catcher Clay Dalrymple was taken out of the game for a pinch-runner, and manager Mauch ran out of catchers. "I put Cookie behind the plate with a one-run lead in the bottom of the ninth," the manager later recalled. "He played as perfect an inning as I've ever seen, and we won the game."

That same season Mauch decided that his infield combination of shortstop Bobby Wine and second baseman Tony Taylor needed a rest. He put Rojas in the line-up at second and Ruben Amaro at shortstop. The two subs played as if they'd been working together for years. The

Playing with the Phillies in '66, Rojas sets up a double play with a throw to first base. Out at second is Giant Tito Fuentes.

Phillies won game after game and took a commanding lead in the National League pennant race. At one point Cookie had 11 hits in 15 times at bat, and his average soared to .538.

During a crucial five-game winning streak, Rojas either hit the key blow or scored the key run in each game. One night against the Los Angeles

Dodgers, he was involved in every run that Philadelphia scored. Late in the season, however, the Phillies ran into a slump and lost the pennant to St. Louis by just one game. It was a disappointing ending to a super season for Rojas.

As good as Cookie's fielding had been that year, it was his hitting that was the real news. The "good-field, no-hit second baseman" finished the season with a fine .291 average. "He's done everything you can ask," said Mauch.

The following season was more of the same for Cookie. In addition to second base, he periodically worked as an outfielder, shortstop, first baseman, and catcher. He made the All-Star team and finished the year with a career-high .303 average.

For the next few years Cookie continued to contribute to the Phils in countless ways. Although his batting never again reached the .300 mark, he became a consistently reliable hitter. In the field, he covered every base, each outfield position, and the shortstop and catcher spots. By 1967 the only part of the diamond he hadn't worked was the mound. And midway through the season he even got a chance to show what he could do there.

On June 30, Philadelphia played a double-header against the San Francisco Giants. The Phillies won an easy 10–3 victory in the opener, but their luck changed drastically in game two. The Giant sluggers completely dominated that contest. By the end of the eighth inning the

Phillies had gone through five pitchers, and the Giants had scored 12 runs on 18 hits. The Philadelphia bullpen was exhausted, and the team was down by nine runs. Clearly the Phils were fighting a losing battle. Mauch took out pitcher number five and sent in his all-purpose utility man—Cookie Rojas. Cookie pitched a more than respectable inning, giving up just one hit and no runs.

Cookie's career was less dramatic for the next two years. Although he continued to be a fine fielder, his batting average fell to just .230. Rojas celebrated his 30th birthday in 1969, and at the end of that season the Phillies decided that his best years were already behind him. On October 7, they traded him to the St. Louis Cardinals in a multi-player deal.

Cookie didn't last long in St. Louis. After only 23 games the Cards dealt him to the Kansas City Royals. What appeared to be the end of the road for Cookie, turned out to be his luckiest break in baseball. Once he hit Kansas City, people reacted to him differently. While the fans in Philadelphia and St. Louis had taken his many skills for granted, those in Kansas City welcomed him enthusiastically. The Royals, only in their second year, needed a man with experience, hustle, and lots of talent. Cookie was their man!

Cookie was as pleased with the Royals as they were with him. "I'm happy I got to a place where I could play again," he said. "When I was in

Cookie slides home safely in a cloud of dust as Yankee catcher Thurman Munson takes a late throw from the outfield.

Philadelphia I played all over the place. It was second base one day, center field the next, and somewhere else next. In St. Louis I wasn't playing at all. They said I was over the hill. But how can you tell when a guy doesn't play? With Kansas City I'm playing in my best position every day. It makes a difference."

Firmly established at second base, Cookie finished the 1970 season hitting .260 in 98 games and solidifying the Royals' defense. But the 1971 season was Cookie's best yet. He teamed up with baseball's smallest man, 5-foot-4 shortstop Freddie Patek, in what manager Jack McKeon called the best double-play combination he ever saw. "You put Cookie and Freddie out there and watch with amazement," said McKeon. "I'd like to have a dozen more like those two. I think they could go out blindfolded. If Cookie flipped one behind his back, Freddie would turn it over. They make bad throws look good."

In June of that season Rojas got his 1,000th major league hit, and in July he played in the All-Star game. He finished the season with an even .300 batting average. And to top it off, he led all second basemen in fielding with a .991 percentage. (During one stretch of 52 games, Rojas didn't make a single error.)

His average dipped to .261 in 1972, but neither Cookie nor the Royals were concerned. Cookie knew how to best utilize his talents. "Seldom can I do the job with one big blow like some power hitters," he explained. "People overlook certain important parts of the game, like moving a runner to third so that he can score on a fly ball—or a hit and run. Maybe you don't get the base hit, but you protect the runner so he can get to second base. These things can cost you in your average and they can cost you chances for RBI's. I'll keep doing them because you have to win games, and there is nothing like winning. Hitting three hundred is great, but some guys might do a better job hitting two-seventy or two-eighty."

Cookie proved his point in 1973. He was named to his third straight All-Star team. Although his average was only .276, he racked up career-highs in RBI's (69), doubles (29), and stolen bases (18) and tied his best campaign with 78 runs scored. And thanks largely to Rojas, the Royals finished the season with an 88–74 record, their best yet.

That year the Rojas-Patek team set a Kansas City record and led the majors with 72 double plays. But despite Cookie's great fielding, his accomplishments were ignored when the Gold Glove, given to the best fielder at each position, was awarded. Rojas was disappointed, but he took the slight in stride.

"Reputations play a big role," he said. "In 1972 I had the highest percentage in the American League, yet I didn't get it. Same thing happened in 1967 and 1968."

After the 1973 season Cookie officially became an American citizen. He also hinted about retiring.

But when the '74 season began, Cookie was back at second base doing all the things he did so well. For the fourth year in a row, he played on the All-Star team. Playing in 144 games, Cookie finished the season with a .271 average and once more led the American League's second basemen in fielding. At the age of 35, Rojas was no youngster—especially by pro baseball's demanding standards. Still, he managed to out-hit, out-field, and just plain out-hustle men ten years younger. And Cookie was still going strong in '75.

"I know that my legs are not as good as they used to be, but I'm not hobbling yet," he said. "I feel I can play at least two more years."

In his years with Kansas City, Cookie spent many hours working with his younger and less experienced teammates. Kansas City skipper Jack McKeon once said Cookie was a manager on the field for the Royals. Rojas made it official late in his career, adding a tenth position to his repertoire—managing a club of his own in a winter league in Venezuela. And there were few men in the game who had more to teach than the multi-talented Cookie Rojas.

BILLY WILLIAMS

During a 1971 visit to the Baseball Hall of Fame in Cooperstown, New York, Chicago outfielder Billy Williams spent hours hunting for a special item—the scorecard of the 1,000th game he'd played during his 1,117 consecutive game streak (a National League record). At the Hall's request, the Cubs had sent the card to Cooperstown to be displayed with the Hall's vast collection of major league mementoes.

Williams sifted through countless items with no success. He finally asked an official where his contribution could be found, only to be told that it had been misplaced. Billy was disappointed—but not exactly surprised. After eleven seasons as one of baseball's greatest unsung heroes, he had come to expect that kind of thing.

Throughout the 1960s and early '70s, Billy's baseball achievements were constantly lost in the shuffle. In more than a decade with the Cubs, he compiled a lifetime batting mark of nearly .300. During those years he swatted an average of nearly 30 home runs per season. Yet even though his homer total (more than 400) exceeded the career marks of such acknowledged long-ball artists as Joe DiMaggio, Yogi Berra, and Ralph Kiner, he was rarely called a super-slugger.

During his prime years, Billy established himself as one of the game's leading RBI men, consistently driving in 90 to 100 runs a season. At one time or another he led the majors in hits, runs, and batting average. And he was near the top in just about every other offensive category. In 1970 he scored 137 runs, more than Hall-of-Famers Stan Musial, Willie Mays, and Hank Aaron ever achieved in one season. Three times he pounded out 200 or more hits in a season.

His impressive contributions at the plate should certainly have put Williams into the superstar category, but more often than not he was completely overlooked by the press and the fans. Quiet and low-key by nature, he never excited a crowd the way Mays did. Nor did he gain the respect and national acclaim that came to Aaron late in the home-run king's career.

Williams was taken for granted in the MVP voting (he never won the coveted award) and in the All-Star balloting (only once was he named to

Billy Williams: the National League's "Iron Man."

the starting team). Even in Chicago, he never got the kind of recognition he so clearly deserved. Although he led the Cubs in almost every department, he was overshadowed by more flamboyant teammates like Ron Santo and Ernie Banks.

After playing with Williams for 13 years, Banks probably knew his teammate's worth better than anyone. "It's too bad that a lot of things Billy does are overlooked," Ernie said in 1973. "He gets so many big hits, makes so many great plays, and yet he's the most underestimated player in the game. He loves the game as much as any of us—he just has a different way of expressing it. Some guys like me go around hollering, but he quietly does it all."

Billy Leo Williams was born on June 15, 1938, in Whistler, Alabama (a suburb of Mobile), to Frank and Jessie Mary Williams. Billy, his three brothers, and one sister, grew up in very poor surroundings. Frank Williams worked on a nearby wharf with Billy's uncle and grandfather, and Mrs. Williams did domestic work for families in the area.

Billy's dad had once been a well-known first baseman for a local team and had played with Satchel Paige, the great Negro League and major league pitcher. After his baseball-playing days ended, Mr. Williams worked long hours and spent a great deal of time away from home, trying to support his family.

With his father away so much, Billy spent a lot

of time with his mother. He often tagged along when she went to work. Billy had to make his own fun because his family did not have much money. His favorite pastimes were fishing and swimming with his brothers in nearby Eight Mile Creek, or feeding the chickens and ducks behind the family home. He spent many happy hours at the nearby Beechcraft airstrip, watching the planes take off and land.

Of course, Billy also played baseball. When his father was home, he would often take Billy out and play catch. While Billy was playing in pick-up games around home, his three older brothers were playing with the Mobile Black Bears, a semi-pro team. One day his brother Clyde got sick, so the other two Williams boys, Franklin and Adolph, convinced their manager to let 13-year-old Billy take Clyde's place. Billy didn't get a hit that day, but the manager recognized his potential and told him to come back when he was older. Three years later Billy became the Black Bears' regular third baseman.

Billy was one of many black youngsters in the Mobile area who would later become big leaguers. Some of the others were Henry Aaron, Willie McCovey, Cleon Jones, Tommie Agee, and Amos Otis. McCovey and Aaron were both friends of Billy's brother Franklin. The three older boys would sit around the Williams' home and talk baseball while Billy just sat there listening.

Although he weighed only 155 pounds in high

school, Billy was a promising all-round athlete. In those days, Mobile County Training School, the local black high school, did not have a baseball team. So Billy tried his luck at football, junior varsity basketball, and track. He was such a good defensive end in football that in his senior year he was offered a scholarship to Grambling, the well-known Louisiana college which produced many pro football stars. But Billy turned down the offer to pursue his baseball career.

At that time Billy was still playing baseball with the Black Bears. But it was his teammate Tommie Aaron (Hank's brother) who was attracting most of the attention from the big league scouts. One of those scouts was Ivy Griffin of the Chicago Cubs. Griffin often came to watch Tommie, who seemed a likely prospect for the Cubs. But after following the team for a short time, Griffin decided that Williams was the real standout.

The Chicago scout was particularly impressed with Billy's beautiful left-handed swing. It wasn't wild or undisciplined like so many others, but smooth and compact—the way the great ones swing. Before too long, Billy signed a contract with the Cub organization. In those days it was very rare for a promising young player to get much money. When Williams signed with the Cubs in 1956 his "bonus" was a cigar for his dad and a one-way ticket to the Cubs' minor league club in Ponca City, Oklahoma—his first stop in professional baseball.

82

Billy was one of only a few black players on the Class D team, and he had a tough time adjusting to his new life away from home. He also had a lot to learn about baseball. He was not the kind of player who succeeded totally on natural ability. He had to work hard. His hitting had always been his strong point, but his fielding left plenty of room for improvement. Don Biebel, Billy's manager at Ponca City, recalled the rookie's first pro game: "He wound up on his stomach trying to field a fly ball."

Billy was eager to improve his fielding. He spent hour after hour, day after day, working on ground balls, trying to get a better jump on fly balls, and strengthening his arm for the long throws to the infield. He eventually became a good—but not great—defensive outfielder. But despite his great improvement, Williams had a difficult time living down his reputation as a poor fielder.

Billy spent 1956 with the Ponca City team but played in only 13 games. The following year, however, he got a chance to show what he could do. He appeared in 126 games and finished the season with a .310 average, 17 homers, 40 doubles, and 95 RBI's.

By the end of '58 Billy had moved up to the Cubs' A team in Burlington, Iowa, and the next year he was promoted to the AA San Antonio team where he had his best season yet. Strangely enough, it was then that Billy almost left baseball. Although he was going strong with a .318 average

Up against the famous ivy-covered wall in Wrigley Field, Billy watches the ball bounce off his glove during a 1962 game.

and 79 RBI's in 94 games, Billy got homesick and began to have frequent stomach problems. One day he asked his roommate to drive him to the train station. He had decided to go home.

Billy spent several days talking things over with his dad and a Cub representative and finally came to grips with his problems. He also got some encouragement from his boyhood hero Hank Aaron, who was already a star with the Milwaukee Braves. Billy went back to San Antonio, and by the end of the season he had advanced to the AAA club at Forth Worth and all the way to Chicago, where he played his first major league game.

Billy started the 1960 season at the Cubs' top farm club in Houston. He smashed the ball with regularity and continued to improve his fielding. His outstanding performance there greatly impressed Rogers Hornsby, the all-time great player and manager. "Get that kid Williams to Chicago as soon as possible," Hornsby told the Cub front office. "No one on the Cubs can swing a bat as well as he can."

The Cubs took Hornsby's advice. Williams was brought up to the big leagues near the end of the season. He made the team for good the next spring and never spent another day in the minor leagues.

Billy got off to a fast start in his first full major league season (1961). His 25 homers and 86 RBI's earned him the National League's Rookie of the

Year award. And the summer of 1962 was even better. He played on the National League All-Star team with Hank Aaron, who did his best to keep the nervous Williams calm. By the end of the season Billy had racked up 22 homers, 92 RBI's, and a .298 average.

Billy kept up that pace in 1963. In 161 games he collected 25 home runs, 95 RBI's, and a .286 average. It was late in that season, on September 22, that Williams began his remarkable consecutive game streak. From that day until September 3, 1970, Williams didn't miss a single game. His "Iron Man" streak was a league record and third in all of baseball history behind the American League's Lou Gehrig and Deacon Scott. Although Williams was proud of his achievement, he later admitted, "If I had to do it over again, I wouldn't!"

"It hurts you," he explained. "It hurts your ballclub. You can't be a hundred percent all the time. In 1964 I was hit on the shoulder and could hardly swing a bat. In 1965 I had a bad back and couldn't bend over. In 1969 I hit myself on the right foot with a foul ball. I could hardly walk. Durocher had me pinch hit to keep the streak alive."

Despite his own words, no one could accuse Williams of hurting his club. For during his streak the Cubs began one of the most successful periods in their history. It started in 1966, when Leo Durocher was hired as manager. He set out to build a winning team around Billy, Chicago legend

Ernie Banks, and all-star third baseman Ron Santo. To get the Cubs out of their losing pattern, Durocher made some important moves. He traded for a young unknown pitcher named Ferguson Jenkins, who later became one of baseball's best hurlers. He acquired pitcher Bill Hands and catcher Randy Hundley from the San Francisco Giants, brought up Ken Holtzman from the minor leagues, and developed shortstop Don Kessinger and second baseman Glenn Beckert into a sparkling double-play combination. By Durocher's second full season the Cubs had jumped from last place to the first division. And just two years later, in 1969, they were serious pennant contenders.

It was a glorious time in Wrigley Field. The team and its accomplishments were the talk of the town. Chicago fans fell in love with their new, exciting Cubs. But while the controversial Durocher, the popular Banks, and the outspoken Santo got most of the headlines, Williams remained in the background. In his own quiet way, however, he was the team's leading batsman.

"You talk about being unnoticed, unheralded, whatever," said veteran play-by-play announcer Milo Hamilton. "You've got to remember that Billy came to Chicago when Ernie Banks was already Mr. Cub . . . then Santo emerged as another star. No matter how you look at it, when the publicity got out, he was always third, whatever he did. I think he was a victim of circumstances."

For the first time in more than 20 years, the Cubs were National League pennant contenders. At the beginning of their surge to the top it was hard to believe that the strong Cub nucleus Durocher had molded in his first couple of years would never win a pennant or divisional title. That, however, is exactly what happened.

The closest the Cubs came to a title was in '69. That year they led the league comfortably until September but faltered in the last days of the season. New York's "Miracle Mets" overtook the slump-ridden and tired Chicagoans in the stretch and went on to win the World Series. Many claimed that it was Durocher, the builder of the machine, who lost the pennant by not resting his regulars, particularly Williams, in the flag drive.

With the 1969 flop hanging over their heads, the Cubs fell short again in 1970, 1971, 1972, and 1973. Where the Cubs failed, however, Billy Williams had one success after another. Those years were his greatest in baseball.

In 1970 he batted .322 and contributed 42 homers, 129 RBI's, and 137 runs to the Cubs' effort. In 1972 he won the league batting championship with a .333 average and the slugging title with a .606 mark. In the process he hit 37 homers and batted in 122 runs.

Although he was named Player of the Year by *The Sporting News*, Billy was overlooked in the Most Valuable Player balloting, just as he'd been in 1970. For the second time in three years he

In a 1971 game, Williams reaches second base just a split second ahead of the Phillies' Denny Doyle.

wound up behind Cincinnati Reds catcher Johnny Bench (who had led his team to the World Series in both years).

After another disappointing season in 1973, the Cub management began a wholesale trading of the men Durocher had assembled with such high hopes. Ernie Banks had already retired, and Ken Holtzman and Bill Hands had been traded. Now Ferguson Jenkins, Ron Santo, Randy Hundley, Glenn Beckert, and outfielder–first baseman Jim Hickman were shuffled off elsewhere. Milt Pappas, a fine pitcher who had joined the Cubs in 1970, was also released. Durocher had already been replaced as manager by Whitey Lockman,

Williams proudly models part of his new uniform after being traded to the world champion Oakland A's in 1975.

and now the Cubs appeared determined to begin a brand new era on the North side of Chicago.

When the 1974 season opened, the only regular holdovers from the Durocher Cubs were Billy and Don Kessinger. Although some of the others had created more attention, it was Billy Williams who was retained to help the younger players build for the future.

Billy's long career with Chicago finally came to an end before the 1975 season got underway. Continuing their youth movement, the Cubs traded him to Oakland. It was a good deal for Billy and the A's. Williams added some extra fire power to Oakland's already explosive line-up. Appearing in 155 games (primarily as a designated hitter), he smashed out 23 homers and drove in 81 runs in '75.

Late in the season the A's clinched the West division crown. It was their fifth such title in as many years—and Billy's first ever. If anyone was as happy about it as Williams, it was Oakland pitcher Ken Holtzman, who had played with Billy in Chicago in the late 1960s and early '70s. Although Holtzman had participated in three world championships with the A's, he saw this title as something special.

"Just seeing that look in Billy's eyes is enough of a reward for me," Holtzman said. "For a guy who has given all that Billy has to baseball, this is a big moment. He's finally on a winner."

MIKE CUELLAR

"I always wanted to be a pitcher," said Mike Cuellar early in his baseball career. "I used to practice every day by myself, throwing home-made baseballs into a basket nailed on a tree—so throwing these brand-new baseballs is easy."

Unfortunately, Mike soon learned that playing professional ball was anything but easy. For nine long seasons (from 1957 to 1965) he toiled in the minors with only a couple of short—and disas-trous—tryouts in the majors.

By the time he played his first full season of big league ball, Mike was 29 years old, an age when many pros have already seen their best years. But in Cuellar's case, it was just the beginning. After brief tours with St. Louis and Houston, Mike joined the Baltimore Orioles in 1969. It was there

Baltimore's Mike Cuellar begins his wind-up.

that he developed into one of the winningest pitchers in baseball.

In his first seven years with the Orioles Mike had four 20-victory seasons, two 18-win seasons, and a grand total of 139 games. He was named to three All-Star teams, was a co-winner (with Denny McLain) of the 1969 Cy Young Award, and was voted the American League's top left-handed pitcher of 1973 by *The Sporting News*.

Miguel "Mike" Cuellar was born in Santa Clara, Cuba, on May 8, 1937. His family worked in the sugar fields, and Mike joined them there after only three years of schooling. As a boy, Mike dreamed of becoming a major leaguer. When he grew up, he enlisted in the Cuban army because it was the only way he knew to escape the sugar fields. More important, he knew he'd be able to play baseball there.

Cuellar was pitching for his army team when he was discovered by a scout from the Havana Sugar Kings, a Triple A team in the Cincinnati Reds' farm system. The Sugar Kings went through a great deal of red tape to get Cuellar out of an army uniform and into a baseball suit.

Cuellar began pro ball in 1957. In his first three seasons in Havana he won a total of 31 games. His earned run averages those years were fine marks of 2.44, 2.77, and 2.80.

Although he was a standout in the minors,

94

Cuellar found he still had a long way to go when the Reds called him up at the end of '59. In his two appearances with the Reds, he was blitzed by the big league sluggers. He pitched only four innings and ran up an unbelievable 15.75 ERA!

Five years went by before Cuellar got another crack at the majors. And by that time he had been released by the Reds and picked up by the St. Louis Cardinals. The turning point in Cuellar's career came in 1964, long after most people had given up on him.

"I was in spring training with Jacksonville, the Cardinals' farm club," Mike recalled. "Reuben Gomez [a former major league pitcher] was on the team, and he knew how to throw a screwball. I started to throw it, and it began breaking better and better. I knew I could make it work."

The screwball turned out to be Cuellar's ticket to the majors. Using the new pitch in 1964, he racked up six wins against only one loss for Jacksonville and compiled a sparkling 1.78 ERA. Later that season the Cards brought him up to St. Louis, but his record there was a disappointing 5–5 with a 4.50 ERA. The following season Mike returned to Jacksonville. By this time he was 28 years old, and the Cards were beginning to think he'd never make it as a major leaguer. Even Mike himself had doubts about his future. After struggling eight years to make it, he was right back where he'd started—in the minors.

"I was pretty gloomy," he admitted later. "But I kept telling myself, 'I'll make it, I'll make it. I have to make it.' "

Back in the minors in '65, Cuellar was going great guns, as usual. Midway through the season he was 9–1 with a 2.51 ERA. But the Cards didn't need a minor league phenom—they needed a professional who could stand up to big league batting. Convinced that Mike would never be that man, they traded him to the Houston Astros.

The Astros brought Mike up to Houston for the rest of the season, and once more he was plagued by his major league jinx. In 25 games with the Astros, Cuellar was credited with only one victory against four defeats.

The Astros were ready to trade Mike away—but no one else wanted him. When the 1966 season got underway, however, the Astros were thankful they'd had no takers. That year everything finally came together for Mike. He turned in one fine performance after another. In his long-awaited first full major league season, he compiled a fine 12–10 record and a superb 2.22 ERA (second only to the great Sandy Koufax among all National League pitchers).

While the St. Louis Cards may have been wishing they'd held on to Cuellar for one more year, many people considered his super '66 season to be a fluke. One expert put it this way: "How old is Mike? Twenty-nine, right? How long has he been pitching, and how many miracles do you have in baseball?"

The following season Mike proved that he was in the majors to stay. His '67 statistics included a winning 16–11 record, a 3.04 ERA, and 203 strike-outs. No one could really explain Cuellar's "overnight" success, but a lot of people tried.

Houston coach Jim Busby said, "I think he feels he belongs on this team. It makes a big difference when a player believes he belongs."

Pitching coach Gordon Jones agreed and added, "Mike knows he has a place on this team. He knows if he has a bad year it doesn't affect his place. He's not going to get pushed back. That is important for a man who spent so many years in the minors."

Then in 1968 Mike's won-lost record slipped to 8–11, despite his excellent ERA of 2.74. Mike had an explanation for his poor showing. "For the first time in my career I wasn't allowed to play winter ball," he said. "The Astros said they wanted me to rest. But I got a sore arm and it affected my pitching all season."

Still, the Astros began to doubt Cuellar's talents once again. His losing season reminded them of his other weaknesses. He was already 31 years old. And he had a habit of losing close games in the late innings. In one game during the 1966 season, he had stopped the Giants without a run until the ninth inning. Then Willie Mays hit a home run to defeat him. Mike lost another 1–0 heart-breaker that year to Los Angeles. Similar things happened to him in 1968. So the Astros decided to make a trade for him.

The last time Mike had been offered for a trade, no one had wanted him. This time the Baltimore Orioles, one of baseball's strongest teams, jumped at the chance to acquire him. The Orioles were eager for the trade because one of their top scouts, Jim Russo, saw Mike's promise.

When Mike got off to a slow start his first spring with the Orioles (1969), the Baltimore management was very concerned. But Russo continued to boost Cuellar. "Listen, you guys haven't really seen Cuellar yet—the one who was striking out twelve and thirteen men a game with Houston," he said. "This guy is more than a pitcher. He's an artist. He has five pitches and complete control of them all."

If there was one thing Mike had learned during his long stay in the minors, it was patience. He wasn't about to panic now. "I knew I'd get runs sooner or later," he said. "There are such good hitters on this club. Best club I've been with."

Before the year was over, Cuellar had more than lived up to his words. He recorded a 23–11 record with a 2.38 ERA and 182 strike-outs. On top of that, he was the co-winner of the league's Cy Young award. The Orioles went all the way to the World Series, where they were defeated by the

**Cuellar cuts down the New York Mets during the opening game of the
1969 World Series.**

New York Mets, four games to one. Baltimore's lone victory came from a masterful performance by Cuellar in the opening game. After countless disappointments and rejections, Cuellar had finally hit his stride.

Mike continued that pace in 1970. He had another slow start and was only 8–5 by the end of June. But then he went on a rampage to finish the season with a league-leading 24–8 record.

Thanks largely to Cuellar's efforts, the Orioles once again made it to the World Series. It was there that Mike erased all doubts about his ability to come through in the big games. Going into the fifth game of the Series, Baltimore led the Cincinnati Reds three games to one. The Orioles needed just one more victory to win the championship, and they were counting on Cuellar to get it for them.

Mike was suffering from a stiff arm that day, but he wasn't going to let that stop him. He had a shaky first inning, giving up three runs on four hits, and was almost lifted by manager Earl Weaver. But then Cuellar got down to business. For the next eight innings he kept the Reds from scoring again, and the Orioles won the game (9–3)—and the Series.

"My arm was stiff and I couldn't get the screwball over after the first inning," Mike said later. "Then I got loose and had great stuff. But I still couldn't throw the screwball. So I went to fastballs and sliders."

Baltimore's four aces (from left to right): Jim Palmer, Dave McNally, Cuellar, and Pat Dobson—all 20-game winners.

In 1971 Cuellar had his third consecutive 20-victory season. He won eleven games in a row from May 12 to the All-Star break and finished up with a 20–9 record. But Mike was only one of many great Baltimore pitchers that year. Teammates

Dave McNally, Jim Palmer, and Pat Dobson all reached the 20-win mark.

Mike's win total went "down" to 18 in both 1972 and 1973, but the following year—when his team needed him most—he was back on top. The Orioles and the New York Yankees were battling it out for the American League East crown. Jim Palmer was sidelined with a sore arm, Dave McNally was in a slump, and Pat Dobson had been traded, so Cuellar was the Orioles' only hope. During that summer Cuellar kept the Orioles going. He halted a five-game losing streak, then a three-game skein, and finally one which lasted four games. He won his last seven starts of the season, easing Baltimore into the playoffs.

Although the Orioles lost the pennant to the Oakland A's, it was an almost perfect season for Cuellar. He made the All-Star team for the third time since 1970, and ended up with a 22–10 record. To top it all off, *The Sporting News* named him the top left-hander in the league. For the first time in his long career, Mike was getting the kind of attention he so clearly deserved.

During that season, Mike's superstitions began to get as much notice as his pitching. Throughout his '74 success, "Crazy Horse," as he was called by his teammates, followed the same routine every day he pitched. For his warm-ups Cuellar would pitch only to coach Jim Frey. Mike would throw him ten to fifteen pitches, from ten feet behind and to the left of the rubber. Then he would return to the rubber for some more practice. While this was going on, Mike wanted catcher Ellie Hendricks to stand by the plate as if he were the batter. It had to be Hendricks—no one else would do.

When the game began, Cuellar would walk to the mound, being careful not to step on the foul line, and pick up a ball which another teammate had placed on the grass. Then he would jog around to the back of the mound (on the first-base side) before striding to the rubber. Next he'd throw seven warm-up pitches—no more and no less. Of the seven, he'd throw three fast balls, two curves, and two screwballs. Mike also claimed it brought him luck to eat Chinese food the night before a game and to wear a blue suit whenever he took an airplane flight.

Cuellar was convinced that these rituals made him the pitcher he turned out to be. Others offered more conventional explanations for his great success.

Frank Robinson, who batted against Cuellar in the mid-1960s and later played with him on the Orioles, witnessed the improvement. "Back then he wasn't that tough," Robinson said. "He was wild. Now he's throwing more strikes with this screwball."

"He's got a fastball, slider, slow curve, and the screwball at several different speeds," added Baltimore pitching coach George Bamberger. "He throws for strikes, and his secret is his great variety. If his screwball isn't working, he can go with something else."

But the real secret of Cuellar's success could be summed up in just a few words—desire, patience, and plain hard work.

BILL MELTON

At the 1971 All-Star game in Detroit, Michigan, baseball's greats assembled to play the 42nd annual classic. There, with Hank Aaron, Willie Mays, and Roberto Clemente, was Bill Melton, the young third baseman of the Chicago White Sox.

"How does it feel to be an All-Star as a rookie?" a reporter asked Melton.

"A rookie!" Melton exclaimed. "I'm in my third season."

The reporter couldn't really be blamed for his mistake. The name Bill Melton was hardly a household word. There'd been no fanfare in 1968 when Melton had made his major league debut with the White Sox. There were no predictions that he would be the next Brooks Robinson at third base. And, with a season's high of twelve home runs in the minor leagues, he hadn't looked like a potential super-slugger. At that time, he was merely expected to back up Pete Ward, an average third baseman who had once been an excellent prospect.

Yet, in the years that followed his debut, Bill established himself as a power hitter and a fine fielder. But just as Melton entered the major leagues in obscurity, he continued to be ignored for most of his playing days. He became a man in constant struggle for recognition. It seemed no matter how hard he tried, or how well he did, he was always in the background.

Life had never been easy for Bill Melton. Born July 7, 1945, in Gulfport, Mississippi, he later moved to San Diego with his family. The Meltons left San Diego in the middle of Bill's high school years. Bill stayed behind with his married sister until he graduated. Money was tight, and Bill had to help with the finances. During the summers he worked on the San Diego docks.

"It was hard work," he recalled. "But I enjoyed it. I worked in boiler rooms. They'd turn the boilers down to about a hundred and sixty degrees, and then we'd put on asbestos suits and go in and clean up. We worked on all kinds of ships—aircraft carriers right down to fishing boats."

During the school year Bill found time to play sports. Oddly enough, he was a three-year letter-

Big Bill Melton: the unknown All-Star.

man in both basketball and football at Durante High, but he never played baseball. He finally went out for the baseball team at Citrus Junior College, but his career ended after only seven games.

"The coach kicked me off the team when I was a freshman," Melton recalled. "He caught me smoking one day and told me not to come back."

Melton began playing in a Sunday league with a Chicago White Sox rookie team. Despite his lack of experience, Bill impressed Sox scout Hollis Thurston. Thurston decided to take a gamble and signed Bill for a small bonus.

In the middle of his sophomore year (1964), Bill left school to begin his pro career as an outfielder at Sarasota, Florida, in the Rookie League. Two years later he was promoted to Appleton, Wisconsin (Class A), where he hit 12 homers and 67 RBI's, maintaining a .284 batting average.

Bill's minor league credentials were respectable but not very special. Yet the White Sox were patient with him. They realized he might take a while to develop because of his late start in organized ball.

Melton was less confident about his chances of making the big leagues, however. "When I was in the minors," he later admitted, "I was so bad in so many things I never thought that I'd really make it."

Melton was as surprised as anyone when Sox manager Eddie Stanky put him on the Chicago spring training roster in 1967. However, Melton soon learned one of the reasons for his quick call-up.

"Stanky told me Mickey Mantle was retiring and he wanted me to see Mantle play at least once," Melton explained. "He told me to just sit on the bench and watch him."

When the regular season started, Bill was sent back to the minors—this time to the AA team in Evansville, Indiana. There he batted .251 and drove in 72 runs in 134 games. Melton spent much of the '68 season in the minors, where he was switched from the outfield to third base. In 34 big league games in Chicago, he drove in 16 runs and batted .266.

Bill got off to a fast start in 1969, his first full major league season. In 157 games he hammered out 23 homers and drove in 87 runs. During one game that season he hit three home runs! He appeared to be the first real slugger brought up through the White Sox farm system in many years. Until Melton came along, the Sox had relied on solid pitching and tough defense. Traditionally a no-hit team, Chicago had brought in power hitters from other teams after they had passed their best years. But players like Del Ennis, Rocky Colavito, Roy Sievers, and Ken Boyer all had very little magic left by the time they reached the South Side of Chicago.

Now, in 1969, here was big Bill Melton—6-foot-1 and 200 pounds—the kind of slugger Sox fans had dreamed about for years. Here was a man, who with one swing of the bat could set off the famous exploding scoreboard at Comiskey Park. Yet after waiting all those years for someone like him, the fans seemed strangely indifferent to Melton.

One reason for this surprising reaction was that the Sox fans wanted a proven superstar, one with magnetism. Melton was quiet and lacked the personality to ignite the fans' imagination. But there was one thing he certainly didn't lack—raw talent. It seemed that Melton and the fans just needed some time to get acquainted.

Unfortunately, Melton couldn't have come up to Chicago at a worse time in the team's history. While the crosstown Cubs were enjoying their finest years in more than two decades, the White Sox seemed stuck in the second division. Their dismal 1969 won-lost record of 68–94 kept them just one step out of the cellar. As a result, not many fans watched the Sox in 1970—the year Melton broke the long-standing team record of 29 homers in a season. Only 495,000 people came to see the Sox play at home that year, and the team finished with a 56–106 record—the worst in either league. With all eyes focused on Wrigley Field and the Cubs, Melton was ignored. And if Melton was inconspicuous in Chicago, he was just about invisible as far as the rest of the country was concerned. He socked out 33 homers and drove in 96 runs, yet nobody knew who he was.

110

"It was the best kept secret in baseball," Melton said. "I knew I hit thirty-three, but I don't think anyone else did. The worst thing in the world is to play on a last-place team because you can do no right."

Despite his fine 1970 effort, Melton was not feeling very confident when the '71 season began. "I picked up one of those magazines that had a rundown on the prospects of all twenty-four clubs," he recalled. "When they came to me, the write-up read: 'A below-mediocre third base-man.'"

It was true, though hardly surprising, that the weakest part of Melton's game was his fielding. After all, he hadn't been switched from the out-field to third base until 1968. Still, the criticism hurt. From that point on, Melton worked hard to beat the rap. He took fielding practice and listened to the advice of his manager and coaches.

When the 1971 season got underway, it was clear that Melton's fielding wasn't the only thing that was improving. That season was a high point for Bill and the whole team. Chuck Tanner was the new manager, and he was determined to turn the failing franchise around. Naturally, he de-pended a lot on Bill Melton, his ace slugger. Melton rose to the occasion, hitting home run after home run. At mid-season Bill was named to the All-Star squad. But, typically, he didn't even get into the game.

As the season came to a close, Melton seemed a

shoo-in for the American League home-run title. But then, after setting a blistering pace, he ran into a slump. By late September he was engaged in a fierce battle for the title with Norm Cash of Detroit and Oakland's Reggie Jackson. By the last day of the season the championship was still up for grabs. Melton batted in the lead-off spot to get an extra turn at bat, and the strategy paid off. He hit his 33rd homer to edge out his rivals, who tied for second place with 32 each.

After the game his teammates poured champagne over his head in celebration, and Melton discussed his late-season slump. "I must have been trying too hard," he admitted. "But Cash and Jackson must have been trying too hard, too."

On his way to becoming the first player in White Sox history to win the home-run title, Melton had also given his team a big boost. That season the Sox climbed from last place in their division to third. And still the fans and newsmen were unimpressed. It could safely be said that Bill Melton was the most unknown home-run champion in history.

The lack of public recognition was beginning to have an effect on Melton. He began to question his own abilities. Manager Tanner tried to reassure him. "Don't say you haven't improved," the skipper said. "You've improved yourself a hundred percent over 1970. You are looking at batting average and home runs. I'm looking at the overall player. You are a much better all-round player than last year."

The 1972 season was a boon for the White Sox but a total disaster for Melton. Just three months after Bill won the '71 home-run title, the White Sox made one of the most important acquisitions in their history. They traded veteran pitcher

After winning the 1971 American League home-run championship, Bill gets a champagne shower from manager Chuck Tanner.

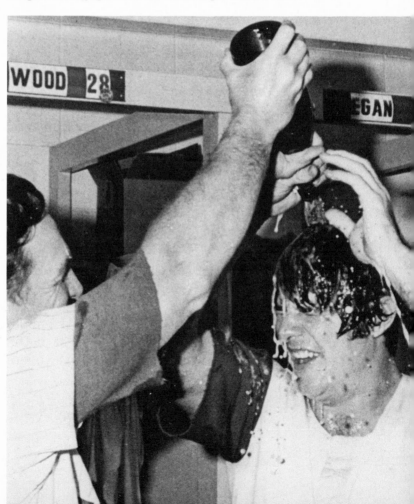

Who's on third? Chicago's Dick Allen (15) gets there first, and Melton (14) has nowhere to go. He was tagged out seconds later.

Tommy John to the Dodgers for slugger Richie Allen. Although Sox fans had been disinterested in Melton, they were delirious about Allen. At long last they had gotten a proven slugger. Allen would be their salvation. With him in the line-up, the pennant could not be far away.

In Allen's shadow stood a young third baseman who just happened to be the American League home-run champion—a man who had racked up 89 homers and 269 RBI's during his first three big league seasons. (Bill had 23 more homers than Hank Aaron had accumulated at that stage in his career.) Melton had just completed a season which would have elevated almost anyone into the superstar category. But with Allen on the roster, and living up to all expectations, Melton was more unsung than ever.

That was only the beginning of Melton's troubles during 1972. Just 57 games into the season, he was stricken by a serious back ailment. There was no doubt that Bill would be out for the rest of the season—if not forever. Without him, the Sox finished the season just five games behind the division champion Oakland A's. It was frustrating for the Sox to think how far they might have gone with Melton in the line-up.

During the winter, Bill underwent demanding therapy to get back in shape for the '73 season. For a while, he spent most of his days and nights lying on the floor to alleviate the pain in his back. He couldn't even sit on a chair. "I was scared to death," he said later. "I didn't know if I'd ever play again. I didn't know if there was any permanent damage. I didn't know if the pain would go away."

Melton's doubts were put to rest as soon as the '73 season began. He could play all right. In fact, in many ways his game was better than ever. After watching Bill play early in the season, manager Tanner commented: "He not only is swinging a quicker bat, but he is better in the field. He is covering more ground. As far as I'm concerned, it is due to the fact that he has taken off some weight."

Melton, too, was pleased with his progress. But he had a different explanation for his success. "Let's face it," he said. "Baseball is a mental game, and confidence means everything. This thing has changed my attitude. I don't fight myself now if I get in a slump or have a bad day. I'm just happy to be here."

Melton had good reason to be happy for the rest of the season. Although he wound up with only 20 homers, he had 87 RBI's and batted .277—his highest major league average ever. He got 155 hits, another personal high, and had fewer strikeouts per time at bat than anyone on the team. He also led the Sox in games played, official times at bat, runs, hits, doubles, and home runs.

Melton's miraculous medical comeback brought him his first public recognition. He was looking forward to more of the same for 1974. Then came the news. Before the season began, the Sox pulled off a gigantic trade with the crosstown Cubs. They acquired veteran third baseman Ron Santo. The big question at the time was: Why do the Sox need two all-star third basemen? As Melton continued to mature, he could be counted on for over 30 home runs and 100 or more RBI's a year. Why, then, did they need another third sacker, one who was obviously on his way down?

The White Sox management explained that Santo and Melton would be alternated as the designated hitter and third baseman. This, they said, would give both players a little more rest. Santo would also spell Richie Allen at first base and put in a little time at second base and in the outfield.

Melton didn't seem to feel threatened by his new teammate. "There is no animosity whatsoever," he said. "Santo will help our club. I've been told I'm still number one at third base, and that is good enough for me. There will be no dissension unless the press starts it."

But when the '74 season began, it became clear that the acquisition of Santo was affecting Melton's performance. By mid-season he was batting under .200 and had just five homers and 30 RBI's—way below his usual pace. Still, manager Tanner insisted that the new system was not hurting Melton. He said that Melton was a pro and would soon snap out of his slump. Bill, however, was less optimistic. "I know," he said. "I've heard that I'm a professional player, that nothing should bother me. But I'm human, too. I just don't have the answer. I'm not going to make excuses."

By the end of the season Melton had taken sole possession of the third base spot and had improved a bit. In August he became the number one

Bill stretches his 6-foot-1 frame to snare a hard-hit grounder.

home-run hitter in White Sox history, hitting his 136th career round-tripper. Because the Sox home-run mark was incredibly low, there was no fanfare. Despite his slow start, Melton managed to finish the season with 21 homers and 63 RBI's. In addition, he led the team in sacrifice flies, walks, total bases, and slugging percentage. Nevertheless, it was a down year for the unlucky third baseman.

Even though Ron Santo retired and Dick Allen was no longer with the White Sox, it seemed likely that Melton would be traded during the off-season. Bill had already said that he wouldn't mind a change of scenery. It turned out that he wasn't traded and he began the 1975 season still hoping to make believers out of the Chicago fans. After another disappointing year, however, the Sox finally dealt Melton to the California Angels.

But Bill Melton's baseball career had already reached heights greater than anyone had expected. In different circumstances he might well have been a superstar. But his abilities were overlooked on a slumping team, overshadowed by glamorous teammates, and threatened by a crippling back injury. These are the makings of a true unsung hero.

RON FAIRLY

"Sometimes I think baseball has too many statistics," said former shortstop Maury Wills. "A guy like me gets a lot of attention for stealing bases. A guy like Sandy Koufax gets all those strike-outs. There isn't enough attention for somebody like Ron Fairly, who does everything well, who worked hard, who isn't really a star but is so much above the average player. You don't hear enough about him."

Wills made that observation in the early 1960s when he and Fairly were teammates on the Los Angeles Dodgers. At the time, Fairly was playing some of his best baseball ever, but it was his famous teammates who received most of the credit.

In 1969, after ten unsung seasons with the

Playing for St. Louis in 1975, Ron Fairly (center) tags Rick Monday of the Chicago Cubs.

star-studded Dodgers, Ron was traded to the expansionist Montreal Expos. There he had a completely different problem. Ron was definitely the big bat in the Expos' line-up, but his contributions didn't seem very important on a club that lost more games than it won. Then in 1975 Ron came to the St. Louis Cardinals. By then, the veteran first baseman was 37 years old, and it was his younger teammates who made the news.

Yet Fairly was a constant contributor, game after game, year after year. In his 16 full major league seasons he compiled a solid .270 batting average, slugged nearly 200 homers, and drove in almost 1,000 runs.

It is not surprising that Ron Fairly became a standout in the major leagues. His father, Carl Fairly, was a fine minor league infielder, and from the start he encouraged Ron to follow in his footsteps. "I was playing catch and swinging a bat before I could walk real well," Ron once said.

Ron was born on July 12, 1938, in Macon, Georgia, where his dad was playing ball. Since Carl Fairly shifted from one minor league team to another, the Fairlys moved often. But when Mr. Fairly retired as a player, the family settled down in Long Beach, California.

Ron became a fine quarterback in football and a good all-round basketball player, but baseball was always his favorite sport. While other boys were playing ball on the sandlots and in school, Ron was playing with semi-pros at the age of eleven. And he played American Legion ball before he entered high school. His coach in Legion ball was none other than Carl Fairly.

"Dad was a fine coach," Ron said. "Actually, he taught me more in the living room, in the bedroom, and in the kitchen than on the field."

At Jordan High School in Long Beach, Ron batted .514 in his senior year and was equally skilled in the field. He earned a scholarship to the University of Southern California, a school which was well known for its fine baseball teams. Ron was such a standout at USC that the Dodgers gave him an $80,000 bonus to sign after his sophomore year.

Ron spent most of his first pro season (1958) with the Des Moines and St. Paul clubs in the Dodger farm system. Late in the year he was called up to Los Angeles. Ron was prepared to sit out the season watching the veterans, but Dodger manager Walt Alston had other ideas. Between games of a double-header, Alston read off the starting line-up. No one was more surprised than Ron when the manager said, "Fairly, right field."

"Go get 'em!" said veteran Carl Furillo, whose place Ron was taking. Dodger center fielder Duke Snider came over to wish him luck and to tell him to relax.

Ron didn't get a hit that day, but that didn't dim his excitement about his major league debut. Ron was especially thrilled with his new teammates. "Gee, the year before I was watching them on TV," he said.

In his next game Ron delivered not one, but three hits. In 15 games that season he batted .283, with two home runs and eight RBI's. And Ron was just as impressive in the field. "The first time he played left field," Alston recalled, "somebody hit a high fly ball. Fairly ran back to the screen and made the catch. He acted like he'd been playing there all his life."

In '59 Ron stayed with the Dodgers as a reserve outfielder. His statistics weren't too impressive, but he did get to play in 118 games—not bad for a 21-year-old only a year away from the college campus. To top it off, the Dodgers won the pennant, and Ron made his first World Series appearance.

In 1960 the Dodgers decided that Ron needed a bit more seasoning, so he spent most of that year in their AAA club in Spokane. There he knocked out 27 homers and drove in 100 runs while batting .303. The next spring he was in the majors for good.

Like so many other "bonus babies," Ron was greeted with mixed emotions by his teammates during those early years. Although they welcomed his abilities, they couldn't help wondering if he was worth all the money he was getting. Fairly, however, soon removed all doubts. He got to the

ballpark early every day, taking extra batting and fielding practice. He showed the veterans that he was more than willing to earn his pay.

Watching him play, Dodger trainer Wayne Anderson was reminded of Ron's dad. Recalling Carl Fairly's days as a minor leaguer, Anderson said, "Carl had the dirtiest uniform on the team. He

The two faces of Ron Fairly: as a 23-year-old Dodger rookie in 1961 (opposite) and a seasoned Montreal veteran in 1970 (above).

worked up a sweat. He got down in the dirt. He played the game right up to the hilt. His son is just exactly like him. He has the dirtiest uniform on this team."

Ron knew only one way to play the game—with lots of hustle. "There are players who work just as hard at the game as I do," he explained. "And there are some who don't. I believe in working hard. I believe in keeping in shape, practicing, learning to do different things, and playing hard. That's the game as I know it."

Ron's dedication paid off in 1961. In 111 games with the Dodgers, he batted .322 and collected 10 home runs and 48 RBI's. He played four positions that year—all three outfield spots and first base. He was especially effective in clutch situations and batted an even .300 as a pinch-hitter.

Fairly was just as cool in the field, as he proved in an early game against the Cubs in Chicago. This time he was playing right field. Chicago's Richie Ashburn hit a long drive, and Ron chased the ball to the famous ivy-covered wall at Wrigley Field. Center fielder Willie Davis, also in pusuit of the ball, was the first to see it. "Don't touch it," Ron shouted. "If we can't find it in the ivy, it's an automatic ground-rule double."

He was right. The hitter, who could have had an inside-the-park home run, returned to second base, and the Dodgers won a close game.

In 1962 Ron became the Dodgers' starting first baseman, playing the outfield only occasionally that year. "I don't care where I play," he said. "Let Mr. Alston decide that. As long as I play, it doesn't matter."

Ron had a fine season, both at first base and at the plate. He finished with 14 home runs, 71 RBI's, and a .278 batting average.

He continued to shine in 1963, hitting .271 with 12 homers and 77 RBI's, and the Dodgers won their first pennant since 1959. In 1964 he had another 70-plus RBI year.

Ron's bat was red hot at the start of '65, and he was hitting .305 by the All-Star break. Unfortunately, a thumb injury cooled him off at mid-season, and he hit a slump. Still, he ended the year with a respectable .274 average and hit the 70 mark in RBI's for the fourth straight season. The Dodgers won the pennant that year, too, and went on to face the Minnesota Twins in the World Series.

Although he had appeared in both the '59 and '63 Series, 1965 marked Fairly's first full-time Series performance. He hit .379 with two home runs, six RBI's, and three doubles, and was a major factor in the Dodgers' victory. If it hadn't been for the great pitching of Koufax, Ron might have won the MVP Award.

"Fairly won so many crucial games for us with his bat," said Dodger pitcher Don Drysdale. "I just came to expect it from him. In late September, when there was no tomorrow, he would always be there with his big hit."

The following season Ron had one of his best years ever, with 14 homers, 61 RBI's, and a .288 average in 117 games. He played in his fourth World Series, but this time Los Angeles was defeated by Baltimore.

Fairly continued to play a vital role in the

Playing with the Dodgers in 1965, Ron connects for a home run.

Dodgers' fortunes until the middle of 1969. Ron was then 31 years old. The Dodgers saw young Wes Parker as their first baseman of the future, and they had a wealth of up-and-coming outfielders. So Fairly was traded to Montreal.

"The Dodgers name had become part of me," Ron said. "But too many good things happened in Los Angeles to allow the trade to spoil it all."

Although he was no longer needed by the Dodgers, Ron was by no means washed up. Montreal, an expansion team that had entered the league in 1969, was badly in need of a man with Fairly's experience and overall knowledge of the game. Ron was more than willing to share his expertise with his younger teammates.

"When I came up to the Dodgers I watched Furillo and Snider and copied their every move," he recalled. "So I owe it to the younger guys on this club to set the same kind of example."

Right from the start, Fairly made his presence known in Montreal. By the end of 1969, after 70 games with the Expos, he had hit .289 with 12 homers and 39 RBI's. In 1970 he continued his fine hitting and was second in fielding percentage among National Leaguer first basemen.

"Ron Fairly is playing first base this year better than anyone I've ever seen play it in the majors," said Montreal manager Gene Mauch. "Especially that first-to-second double play. It is one of the toughest plays in the book. I defy anyone else to do it like he can."

Ron had two more good years in 1971 and '72, but the '73 season was really special. He got off to an incredible start and was batting .429 by the end of April. By the All-Star break he was at .307 and was named to the squad for the first time in his career. Ron maintained his pace for the rest of the season. Not coincidentally, that year the Expos began to look like real contenders in the National League East, finishing the season just three-and-a-half games out of first place.

Injuries slowed Ron down in 1974, and he had a below-par season. At the end of the year the Expos decided that a youth movement was in order. To bring up some promising youngsters from their farm system, they had to let go of such proven performers as Ron, Willie Davis, Ken Singleton, and Ron Hunt.

Fairly was snapped up by the St. Louis Cardinals, who had just missed out on the '73 and '74 Eastern Division titles. They hoped that Fairly could make the difference in '75.

Although the Cards again fell short of their goal in '75, Ron did everything that could have been expected of him. The 37-year-old veteran finished his 17th full major league season with a fine .301 batting average, 6 home runs, and 37 RBI's in 107 games.

"Baseball's been my whole life," Ron said early in his career. "I've been around ballparks and clubhouses and ballplayers as long as I can remember. I played kids' baseball and high school baseball and college baseball, and now I'm playing pro baseball. I love the game. I think right now I want to stay in it all my life. If you told me I'd still be at it fifty years from now, I'd be happy."

In 1975, almost two decades later, Ron Fairly was still at it—and the way he was playing, he had good reason to be happy.

TONY PEREZ

In his first eleven full seasons with the Cincinnati Reds, first baseman Tony Perez hit 20 or more home runs eight times, including a career-high of 40 in 1970. He drove in over 100 runs six times and hit the 90-plus mark on three other occasions. And during that period he maintained an excellent .285 batting average. There were few stars who could boast such impressive statistics—but unfortunately for Tony, many of them were his teammates.

Although Perez's batting average was one of the most consistent in baseball, he couldn't come close to Pete Rose in that department. Rose batted over .300 nine years in a row. Pete also had the advantage of being a homegrown Ohio boy. Perez couldn't match Rose's records—or his romance with the Cincinnati fans.

Cincinnati's Tony Perez keeps his cool during a tense moment in a 1972 game.

Tony was a powerful home-run and RBI hitter, but in both cases he was edged out by catcher Johnny Bench. Twice Bench led the league in home runs, and he was the RBI champ three times. When the sportswriters weren't praising Rose, they were praising Bench.

Perez himself had nothing but good things to say about his more famous teammates. And he never let his own lack of publicity get him down. "I just try to hit," he explained. "They pay me enough for what I do. I wanted to win, and Bench came along and we began to win. I have no envy of Bench. Some guys get publicity—some guys don't. I just try to do my job."

His teammates may have overshadowed him when it came to batting average, home run, and RBI titles, but there was one title nobody could take away from Perez—that of "Mr. Clutch." When the Reds needed a late-inning run to tie up a game or win it, Tony was their man. Whenever the going got rough, they looked to Perez. As former Cincinnati manager Dave Bristol put it, "If a game goes long enough, Tony Perez will find a way to win it."

A native of Camaguey, Cuba, Tony was born in the town of Ciego de Avila on May 14, 1942. "As a kid, everything—my whole life—was baseball," he recalled. "There was school, work, and baseball—and baseball was what you lived for.

"When I was fourteen, I was out working with

my daddy in the sugar factory. You could hear the noise of the machines all the time. It made me nervous. I don't like that work. I used to kid my mother about it and say, 'I'm going to be a professional baseball player.'

"My mother would say, 'You going to be like your daddy and your brother, work in the factory.'

"My sister and brother would say, 'You not going to play any professional baseball. You too skinny.' That worried me."

Tony was a tall, slender 17-year-old shortstop for a sugar factory team when the Cincinnati Reds scouted him. Fidel Castro had recently taken over the Cuban government, and he was not friendly with the United States. Tony realized that if he left Cuba to play ball in the United States, there was a chance he might not be allowed to return home. Tony loved baseball and had always wanted to be a pro. But he also loved his family very much. It was a tough decision to make, but Tony finally signed with Cincinnati.

In his first professional season (1960) at Geneva, New York, Tony showed great potential. The following year he belted 27 homers, drove in 132 runs, and hit for a blistering .348 average.

Although Tony moved up a notch in the Reds farm system in 1962, it was a bad year for him. After spending the winter in Cuba, he had trouble leaving the country and was late for spring training camp. He made up for lost time, however, batting .292 with 18 homers and 74 RBI's in his first 100 games. Then the season came to a sad and premature end. Tony broke his leg and spent the rest of the season and that winter in Cuba. While Perez was recuperating at home he couldn't help worrying about his future. He had no way of knowing whether he'd ever be able to play pro ball again.

Although the Reds were sympathetic, they were not particularly worried about Tony's condition. Despite his good early showing, Perez was just one prospect among many talented Red hopefuls. In fact, during his first season at Geneva, Tony had been moved from second base to third to make room for a young kid named Pete Rose. The Reds had given Rose a big bonus, and they couldn't afford to keep him on the bench. They had invested very little in Tony, however, so they had little to lose if he didn't make it.

But Tony bounced back in 1963 and had a fine year in Macon (Georgia) and San Diego. He later recalled that season as a turning point in his career. "I played for Dave Bristol that year in Macon," he said. "At the end of the season Dave told me I was too skinny. I should go home and put on more weight. So all winter I eat rice and beans."

Tony spent the off-season at a friend's home in North Carolina and returned to training camp 40 pounds heavier. Now Bristol told him to lose some weight, but Tony just laughed. At 6-foot-2 and 200 pounds, Perez was an impressive sight.

Perez was bigger and better than ever in '64. Playing on the Reds' top farm team, he compiled a .309 batting average with 34 home runs and 107 RBI's. Near the end of that season he was brought up to Cincinnati, where he made the team for good.

Throughout 1965 and '66 Perez was platooned at first base with veteran Gordy Coleman. Although he didn't get to play every day, Tony made the most of his chances with an awesome display of power. In one 1965 game against the Braves in Milwaukee, he hit a tape-measure home run into the left-center-field bleachers, a feat never before accomplished in that stadium. In Philadelphia he knocked one on top of the stands in Connie Mack Stadium. And in Cincinnati he hit a towering homer over the Crosley Field scoreboard. Perez was so impressive that many experts were boosting him for the league's Rookie of the Year award despite his part-time status.

By 1967 Tony had more than earned a regular place in the line-up. But the Reds had another promising young first baseman, Lee May, and they wanted to play him, too. So Tony was switched back to third base. In his first full-time season, Tony swatted 26 home runs and 102 RBI's, averaging .290 at the plate.

A highlight of that season was Tony's first All-Star appearance. Tony's big moment got off to a strange start. The game was being played in Anaheim, California. When Tony and his wife

139

Playing first base in 1965, Tony takes a throw from the pitcher in an attempt to pick off Philly baserunner Ruben Amaro.

went to check into their hotel, they found that there'd been a mix-up. No reservation had been made for them. Things were quickly resolved, and the Perezes were put up in the Presidential Suite —the most luxurious rooms in the place.

There was no mix-up about the game, however. Tony was the undisputed hero there. With the score tied 1–1 going into the 15th inning, the longest All-Star classic on record ended as Perez

140

powdered a long home run for the National League. That was just one of a long line of clutch performances Tony turned in throughout his career.

The 1968 season was another banner year for Perez. He blasted 18 homers, drove in 92 runs, and hit a solid .282. In 1969 Tony outdid himself. He ranked fourth in home runs (with 37) and third in RBI's (122) among all National Leaguers. He also boosted his average to .294. Yet Tony was almost unnoticed behind Rose, who won his second straight batting crown, and Lee May, who bettered Tony's home run total with 38.

Tony started off the 1970 season second to no one. In the month of April alone, he socked ten home runs, tying the big league standard set by Frank Robinson. That same month, Tony batted a sizzling .450. He finished the season with a career-high .317 average and 40 home runs (another personal milestone). His 129 RBI's tied him for second place in the league in that department.

With those kinds of statistics, Perez should have been a strong candidate for the league's Most Valuable Player award. But he wasn't the only one having a great season in 1970. That year teammate Johnny Bench won both the home-run and RBI titles—and then the MVP.

With Perez, Bench, and Rose all in top form, the Reds went all the way to the 1970 World Series. Although they lost the championship to the Baltimore Orioles, the Reds had clearly begun a new era. In the years that followed, Cincinnati became one of baseball's strongest teams and a perennial contender in the post-season playoffs.

In 1972 Lee May was traded to Houston, and Perez moved back to first base. The Reds entered the World Series for the second time in three years. Although Perez batted an incredible .435 in the Series, the Reds were defeated again, this time by the Oakland A's.

After the season Tony went back to Cuba—his first visit home since 1963. Tony got a hero's welcome. His friends and family were amazed. The last time they'd seen him, Tony had been a skinny little shortstop. Now he was a huge first baseman. In his native country, Tony was truly number one.

"All my old friends, the kids I played with when I was young, were all waiting for me. They all wanted to talk," he told a reporter upon his return to the United States. "They have so many arguments about baseball and they want me to answer them."

In 1973 Perez continued to shine. After the All-Star break he and the Reds made another successful run for the division title. In one 38-game stretch, Tony hit .401. In an eleven-game streak in August, he hit .359, with two hits in each game. From August 3 to September 2, when the wear and tear of the season were beginning to take their toll on many of the best players, Tony hit safely in 26 of 27 games.

Perez slides home safely during the 1972 World Series against the Oakland A's.

Perez was at his best when it counted most—against the other division contender, the Los Angeles Dodgers. Perez's clutch performances became routine. He batted .384 against the Dodgers, with six home runs and 18 RBI's. He hit two home runs off Dodger Claude Osteen for a 4–1 Reds victory in May. In July he hit a two-run homer off Jim Brewer to beat Los Angeles 4–2. In September a three-run homer, his fifth hit in the game, gave the Reds a 4–1 win.

The Reds finished on top in the N.L. West division, and Perez wound up with a .314 average, 27 home runs, and 101 runs driven in. "I am more comfortable at the plate with men on base," he said, explaining his excellent RBI total. "Maybe I concentrate harder. I think I bear down a little more when I know there is someone out there for me."

Perez's importance to the Reds was clearly demonstrated during the '73 playoffs against the Eastern champion Mets for the pennant. Perez ran into a slump and batted only .091 in the playoffs. Without Perez to hit the key blows, the Reds bowed to the Mets and lost the chance to enter another World Series.

In 1974 Tony regained his superior consistency. He had another great year with 28 homers and 101 RBI's. His clutch hitting was as spectacular as usual. The Reds, however, did not do as well. They ran into a much improved Dodger team and lost the division title.

Tony Perez: Cincinnati's "Mr. Clutch."

At the end of the season the Reds decided to trade Perez. They had a promising young first baseman, Dan Driessen, who was developing into a super-slugger. Driessen had played third base during the season, but the Reds knew he'd do better at his natural position. Therefore, they made it known that the 32-year-old Perez was available for a trade.

As it turned out, Perez was not traded. The Reds could not get what they wanted for him, so he remained in Cincinnati. His narrow escape made Perez more determined than ever to succeed, and he got off to a fast start in 1975.

It was a super season for both Tony and the Reds. Cincinnati wound up with another National League pennant, while Perez racked up 109 RBI's, 20 home runs, and a .282 average. But it was in the World Series, against the Boston Red Sox, that Perez really proved his worth.

After four games the teams were all tied up with two victories apiece. Then in game five Tony belted out back-to-back home runs to pace the Reds to a 6–2 victory.

Boston came back to win game six in a twelve-inning cliff-hanger, so the world championship came down to the seventh—and final—game. When Boston took an early lead (3–0) in that contest, it began to look as if the Reds would once again fall short of the championship. But in the sixth inning, Perez came through with a two-run homer that put Cincinnati right back in the ballgame. An inning later Pete Rose provided the game-tying RBI with his tenth base hit of the Series, and in the top of the ninth Joe Morgan drove in the winner. For the first time in 35 years, the Cincinnati Reds were world champions.

Not surprisingly, Rose was named MVP. But no one could deny that Tony Perez, with seven big RBI's (the highest total for either team), had retained his title of "Mr. Clutch."

INDEX

Page numbers in italics refer to photographs.

Aaron, Henry, 78, 81, 85, 86, 105, 115
Aaron, Tommie, 82
Agee, Tommy, *44*, 81
Allen, Dick, *114*, 117, 120
Alston, Walter, 124, 128
Amarillo, Texas, minor league team, 30
Amaro, Ruben, 68
Anderson, Wayne, 126
Ashburn, Richie, 128
Aspromonte, Bob, 31, 34
Atlanta Braves, 46, 48, 49, 50
  see also, Milwaukee Braves
Atlanta Stadium, 46
Austin, Texas, minor league team, 42

Baltimore Orioles, 18, 19, 59, 92, 94, 98, 129, 141

Bamberger, George, 104
Bando, Sal, 11, 12
Banks, Ernie, 80, 87, 90
Beckert, Glenn, 87, 90
Bench, Johnny, 51, 89, 136, 141
Berra, Yogi, 53, 78
Biebel, Don, 83
Binghamton, New York, minor league team, 56
Blasingame, Don, 67
Bonds, Bobby, 62
Boston Red Sox, 23, 146
Boyer, Ken, 109
Brewer, Jim, 144
Bristol, Dave, 138
Bulganzio, Dominic, 29
Burdette, Lew, 48
Burlington, Iowa, minor league team, 83
Busby, Jim, 97

California Angels, 120
Campaneris, Bert, 11
Capra, Buzz, 40, 48, 49
Casanova, Phil, 46
Cash, Norm, 112
Castro, Fidel, 67, 137
Cedeno, Cesar, 37
Chicago Cubs, 36, 77, 82, 128
Chicago White Sox, 105, 108, 110, 112–116, 118, 120
Cincinnati Reds, 18, 19, 64, 67, 94, 95, 100, 134–147
Clemente, Roberto, 105
Cleveland Indians, 56
Colavito, Rocky, 109
Coleman, Gordy, 139
Comiskey Park, 110
Connie Mack Stadium, 139
Crosley Field, 139
Cuellar, Mike, 59, 92–104
  photos of, *93, 99, 101*

Dalrymple, Clay, 68
Davis, Willie, 128, 132
D'Bardini, Lou, 28
Denver, Colorado, minor league team, 42
Des Moines, Iowa, minor league team, 124
Dickey, Bill, 53
DiMaggio, Joe, 78
Dobson, Pat, *101,* 102
Doyle, Denny, *89*
Driessen, Dan, 146
Drysdale, Don, 129
Duncan, Dave, 15
Durocher, Leo, 86, 87, 88

Ennis, Del, 109
Evansville, Illinois, minor league team, 109

Fairly, Ron, 121–133
  photos of, *122, 126, 127, 130*
Fingers, Rollie, 15
Fisher, Eddie, 43
Fisk, Carlton, 51
Fort Worth, Texas, minor league team, 85
Frey, Jim, 102
Fuentes, Tito, *69*
Furillo, Carl, 124

Gehrig, Lou, 86
Griffin, Ivy, 82

Hamilton, Milo, 87
Hands, Bill, 87, 90
Harrelson, Ken, 56
Hatton, Grady, 31
Havana, Cuba, minor league team, 94
Havlicek, John, 41
Helms, Tommy, 37
Hendricks, Ellie, 103
Hickman, Jim, 90
Holtzman, Ken, 90, 91
Hornsby, Rogers, 85
Houk, Ralph, 56, 59
Houston Astros, 24, 25, 26, 30, 92, 96, 97, 98
Howard, Elston, 53
Hundley, Randy, 87, 90
Hunt, Ron, 132
Hunter, Catfish, 12, 23, 62

Illinois Wesleyan University, 28

Jackson, Reggie, 11, 12, 15, 17, 20, 112

Jacksonville, Florida, minor
league team, 42, 95
Jenkins, Ferguson, 87, 90
John, Tommy, 114
Jones, Cleon, 81
Jones, Gorden, 97

Kansas City Athletics, 15, 23
see also Oakland Athletics
Kansas City Royals, 63, 71, 74
Kent State University, 54
Kessinger, Don, 87, 91
Kiner, Ralph, 78
Koufax, Sandy, 96, 129
Kroc, Ray, 24

Lau, Charley, 17, 18
Lockman, Whitey, 90
Los Angeles Dodgers, 20, 69, 98,
121, 124–133, 144
Louisville, Kentucky, minor
league team, 42

Macon, Georgia, minor league
team, 138
Mantle, Mickey, 109
Mauch, Gene, 68, 70, 71, 131
May, Lee, 37
Mays, Willie, 78, 97, 105
Mazeroski, Bill, 41
McCook, Nebraska, minor
league team, 42
McCovey, Willie, 81
McKeon, Jack, 74, 76
McLain, Denny, 94
McNally, Dave, 101, 102
Melton, Bill, 105–120
photos of, 107, 113, 114, 119
Menke, Denis, 19

Millan, Felix, 22
Milwaukee Braves, 38, 42, 43, 85,
139
see also Atlanta Braves
Minnesota Twins, 129
Mobile Black Bears, semi-pro
team, 81
Monday, Rick, 122
Montreal Expos, 123, 131–133
Morgan, Joe, 147
Munson, Thurman, 51–62
photos of, 52, 55, 58, 61, 72–73
Musial, Stan, 78

New York Giants, 97
New York Mets, 20, 36, 46, 88,
100
New York Yankees, 51–56,
102
Niekro, Joe, 40
Niekro, Phil, 38–50
photos of, 39, 44, 47

Oakland A's, 11, 17–23, 91, 102,
115, 142
Oklahoma City, minor league
team, 31
Osteen, Claude, 144
Otis, Amos, 81
Owens, Jim, 68

Paige, Satchel, 80
Palmer, Jim, 101, 102
Pappas, Milt, 90
Parker, Wes, 131
Patek, Freddie, 74, 75
Perez, Tony, 134–147
photos of, 135, 140, 143, 145
Philadelphia Phillies, 63, 68, 70

Ponca City, Oklahoma, minor
  league team, 82
Pries, Don, 15
Pruette, Jerome, 54

Rader, Doug, 24–38
  photos of, *26, 29, 32–33, 35*
Richmond, Indiana, minor
  league team, 45
Robinson, Brooks, 36, 105
Robinson, Frank, *58,* 103, 141
Rojas, Cookie, 63–76
  photos of, *65, 69, 72–73*
Rose, Pete, 27, 134, 138, 147
Rudi, Joe, 11–23
  photos of, *13, 16, 21, 22*
Ruiz, Chico, 64
Russo, Jim, 98

St. Louis Cardinals, 70–74, 92,
  95, 96, 123
St. Paul, Minnesota, minor
  league team, 124
San Antonio, Texas, minor
  league team, 83
San Diego, California, minor
  league team, 138
San Diego Padres, 24, 37, 46
San Francisco Giants, 70
Santo, Ron, 80, 87, 90, 116, 117
Sarasota, Florida, minor league
  team, 108
Savannah, Georgia, minor
  league team, 66
Scott, Deacon, 86
Scott, George, *61*
Sievers, Roy, 109
Snider, Duke, 124

Southern California, University
  of, 124
Spahn, Warren, 48
Stanky, Eddie, 108
Streeter, Jerry, 14
Syracuse, New York, minor
  league team, 56

Tanner, Chuck, 111, 112, *113,*
  116, 117
Taylor, Tony, 68
Tenace, Gene, 19
Thurston, Hollis, 108
Triandos, Gus, 68

Virdon, Bill, 60, 62

Walker, Harry, 34
Ward, Pete, 106
Watson, Bob, 37
Wausau, Wisconsin, minor
  league team, 66
Weaver, Earl, 100
Wilhelm, Hoyt, 43, 49, 50
Williams, Adolph, 81
Williams, Billy, 77–91
  photos of, *79, 84, 89, 90*
Williams, Clyde, 81
Williams, Dick, 14
Williams, Franklin, 80, 81
Williams, Jessie, 80
Wills, Maury, 121
Woodling, Gene, 54
Wrigley Field, 87, 110

Yastrzemski, Carl, 17